PRAISE F

"*Crossing the Chasm* is a masterful summation of the authors' years of experience helping Latter-day Saints understand the biblical gospel of grace. Engagingly written, it will help any Christian feel equipped to have fruitful faith conversations with Mormons. The book demonstrates that, by staying focused on the most important things, you don't have to be an expert in Mormonism to be an effective witness.

Witnessing to Mormons can feel like a daunting task, and efforts to do so often run aground. *Crossing the Chasm* does a masterful job in avoiding typical pitfalls to equip ordinary Christians for effective conversations with Latter-day Saints. This is a must-read book for anyone who wants to share the good news of God's grace with Mormons.

Crossing the Chasm is an excellent resource for helping ordinary Christians fruitfully share the gospel with Latter-day Saints. But I am impressed about the value of this book for helping former Mormons understand the powerful life implications of their new identity in Jesus. I plan to use and promote this book widely."

—**Ross Anderson**
Author of *Understanding Your Mormon Neighbor*
Director of Utah Advance Ministries

"Lots of good pointers."

—Sandra Tanner
Utah Lighthouse Ministry

"There is a great chasm for anyone who tries by their efforts to live with God forever. With this book, Mark and Jon not only show us how that chasm exists for our LDS friends but also how God provided the one and only bridge to bring all of us to live with Him forever."

—Jon Klein
Pastor in Layton, Utah

CROSSING THE CHASM

Helping Mormons Discover the Bridge to God

MARK J. CARES
JON LEACH

Copyright © 2020 Mark J. Cares & Jon Leach

Published by Truth in Love Ministry. All rights reserved.

Illustrations by Lucas Boehm.

All Scripture quotations, unless otherwise indicated, are taken from The Holy Bible, New International Version® NIV® Copyright © 1973 1978 1984 2011 by Biblica, Inc.™ Used by permission of Zondervan. All rights reserved worldwide.

Scripture quotations marked (ESV) are from the ESV® Bible (The Holy Bible, English Standard Version®), copyright © 2001 by Crossway, a publishing ministry of Good News Publishers. used by permission. All rights reserved.

All rights reserved worldwide. No part of this publication may be reproduced, distributed, or transmitted in any form or by any means, including photocopying, recording, or other electronic or mechanical methods, without the prior written permission of the publisher, except in the case of brief quotations embodied in critical reviews and certain other noncommercial uses permitted by copyright law.

ISBN: 978-0-0074187-8-1

Lord Jesus, you have called me to be your witness. I confess too often your message is muted because I think of myself. So, send the Spirit to fix my eyes on you. Move me to marvel at your amazing grace which reached me. Restore to me the joy of your salvation. Then, overflowing in confidence that can only come from you, send me out.

Give me your eyes to see the opportunities all around. Give me your heart to understand you shed your blood for each soul. Give me patient ears to listen to the hurting. Then, place your powerful Word on my tongue so many more might discover the great things you have done for them. Prepare me, Lord, for my mission. Amen.

TABLE OF CONTENTS

Preface | 9
Sources of LDS Authority | 15
Introduction | 17

PART ONE: HOW WIDE IS THE CHASM? | 19
Chapter 1: Who God Is | 23
Chapter 2: Who We Are | 33

PART TWO: HOW TO CROSS THE CHASM | 47
Chapter 3: The Father's Plan | 51
Chapter 4: The Son's Role | 65
Chapter 5: The Spirit's Work | 79

PART THREE: RETURN TO REACH MORE | 93
Chapter 6: Answering Uncertainty | 97
Chapter 7: Dropping the Baggage | 113
Chapter 8: Walking Together | 127

Additional Resources | 139
Index | 147
Bibliography | 151
About the Authors | 157

PREFACE

A sea change has occurred in Mormonism since Mark wrote *Speaking the Truth in Love to Mormons*. 20 years ago, LDS members regularly referred to Bruce R. McConkie's *Mormon Doctrine* to explain their beliefs. They routinely quoted Spencer W. Kimball's *The Miracle of Forgiveness*. The LDS Church sharply distinguished itself from Christianity.

It also had no problem being called Mormon. At the October 1990 General Conference, President Gordon B. Hinckley, who would later become their prophet, gave a talk entitled "*Mormon Should Mean 'More Good.'*" He approvingly quoted a missionary: "While I'm thankful for the privilege of being a follower of Jesus Christ and a member of the Church which bears His name, I am not ashamed of the nickname *Mormon*." Hinckley ended his talk by saying:

> When people speak of us by the name of this book, they will compliment us, if we will live worthy of the name, remembering that in a very real sense *Mormonism* must mean that greater good which the Lord Jesus Christ exemplified. (52)

It's different today. Most Mormons now see themselves as Christians and become agitated when they aren't considered as such. *Mormon Doctrine* and *The Miracle of Forgiveness* are no longer popular. And their president has told them to no longer identify themselves as Mormon or LDS. Thus, for example, the Mormon Tabernacle Choir is now called the Tabernacle Choir at Temple Square.

But the changes have all been cosmetic. LDS doctrine, especially the central issues of sin and salvation, remains the same. At its core, Mormonism persists as a non-Christian religion. This is more difficult to see, however, as Mormons act and talk increasingly like Christians. In fact, even many Christians now regard Mormonism as a Christian religion.

Because Mormonism's basic teachings haven't changed, the principles in *Speaking the Truth in Love to Mormons* are still relevant. The stresses Mormons experience have remained remarkably consistent over the years. The language differences persist. Most importantly, Mormons still desperately need us to speak the truth to them in love.

Sometimes this surprises Christians because many Mormons are leaving the LDS Church. Much of this exodus is a result of the Internet. Before its widespread use, Mormons could remain quite isolated from any criticism of Mormonism. Now, however, a wealth of information about Mormonism's history and doctrine is at their fingertips. After reading this information, some become disillusioned about their church.

But a shockingly small percentage become Christian! The majority become agnostic, i.e. they believe there is a God but feel it's impossible to discover who the real one is. Some studies have placed the number of agnostic former Mormons as high as two out of three. It's not that difficult to see why. They focus almost entirely on the problems of Mormonism and never hear the true message of the gospel. They need somebody to proclaim Christ to them!

The need to share Jesus with Mormons is as great as it ever has been. That is why we decided to write this book. It's not a replacement for *Speaking the Truth in Love to Mormons*. Rather, it builds on it. Many of the topics addressed in *Speaking* are not dealt with here. For example, it has a thorough overview of the LDS plan of salvation. It also takes a systematic look at LDS doctrine. This book does neither. Instead, we only touch on the topics which are relevant to helping Mormons understand the biblical way of salvation.

During the last 20 years, our ministry has also undergone a tremendous change. When Mark wrote *Speaking*, Truth in Love Ministry did not exist. Now it has a worldwide presence, a staff of about a dozen and hundreds of volunteers around the world. We have spoken with thousands of LDS members and equipped tens of thousands of Christians to witness to Mormons. We have learned much from these interactions—lessons we share in this book. It is our prayer they will help you share Jesus with Mormons.

There are a few other points which we need to address before we dive in. The first is our use of "Mormons" and "LDS." We use these names not out of spite of President Nelson's statement, but solely for practical purposes. It is beyond awkward to write, "the members of the Church of Jesus Christ of Latter-day Saints" every time we refer to them. Most LDS members don't even do that. Even official LDS sources still commonly use LDS or Latter-day Saints.

By the way, even using LDS or Latter-day Saints go against the reason President Nelson cited for using the full name. In the following quote, note how he emphasizes both the absence and disregarding of

Jesus' name:

> When it comes to nicknames of the Church, such as the "LDS Church," the "Mormon Church," or the "Church of the Latter-day Saints," the most important thing *in* those names is the *absence* of the Savior's name. To remove the Lord's name from the Lord's Church is a major victory for Satan. When we *discard* the Savior's name, we are subtly *disregarding* all that Jesus Christ did for us—even His Atonement. ("The Correct Name of the Church" 88)

It is true that many LDS members are no longer calling themselves Mormon. The reason we retain it is, again, a practical one. Simply put, it is the name most Christians associate with them. Almost without fail when we use LDS outside of the Intermountain West, some Christians ask us who we are talking about. On the other hand, most Christians understand when we use the name Mormon.

On a different topic, we continue the procedure established in *Speaking* of citing only current and authoritative sources. This is important because many LDS members don't know or don't agree with official LDS teaching. At times, therefore, we need to show them what their church is currently teaching. One example of an official source is their many church manuals. We only quote manuals currently used in the LDS Church. (This holds true even if their copyright is older.)

We especially focused on quoting recent General Conference talks since the LDS Church continues to equate them with scripture. "The inspired words of our living prophets become scripture to us.

Their words come to us through conferences, the *Liahona* or *Ensign* magazine and instructions to local priesthood leaders" (*Gospel Principles* 48). These conference talks are always printed in the May and November issues of their monthly magazine, *Ensign*. You will see those issues quoted frequently. (In January 2021, *Ensign* received a new name, *Liahona*. Liahona was a ball-like compass in the Book of Mormon.)

We highly encourage the use of the King James Version (KJV) of the Bible when witnessing to Mormons. It is their official translation. (Contrary to what many people think, they have not altered it.) In this book we usually use the New International Version (NIV) for ease of understanding. If you quote Bible passages to your LDS friends, remember to quote them in the KJV.

Finally, our ministry has created numerous written and video resources to help you witness. They are described in the appendix. We encourage you to explore them.

SOURCES OF LDS AUTHORITY

MORMON SCRIPTURES

Book of Mormon
- Referred to as "the keystone of our religion"
- Supposedly translated by Joseph Smith from golden plates
- Supposedly tells the story of the Nephites and Lamanites in early America

Doctrine and Covenants
- Abbreviated as D&C
- Supposed revelations received mainly by Joseph Smith
- Source of many of Mormonism's unique beliefs

Pearl of Great Price
Consists of five brief documents:
- Book of Moses
- Book of Abraham
- Joseph Smith – Matthew
- Joseph Smith – History
- The Articles of Faith

The Bible
- "We believe the Bible to be the word of God as far as it is translated correctly" (8th Article of Faith)
- Their official version is the King James Version

WORDS OF THEIR LIVING PROPHET

- The President of the LDS Church is also considered the "Living Prophet." Although LDS apostles are also called prophets, only the president has the title "Living Prophet."
- Mormonism places his words on the level of scripture
- Disagreement about which of his statements rise to this level

GENERAL CONFERENCES

- Held twice a year (1st weekend in April and 1st weekend in October)
- Consists of talks primarily given by General Authorities (Prophet, Apostles, Seventies)
- Members are encouraged to study them

OFFICIAL CHURCH MANUALS

- Published by the LDS Church
- Widespread disagreement about how authoritative they are

INTRODUCTION

Every religion recognizes there is a chasm between God and mankind. The concept of "god" demands it—god is always defined as a higher being or power. If there was no chasm, there would be no reason for religion.

Religion is all about bridging the chasm. Each religion lays out its own way of accomplishing this feat. However, there are essentially only two ways. One way is to put the burden on humans. In some way and to some degree, it is up to them to cross the chasm. Religions adhering to this pattern only differ by what they prescribe. Some emphasize meditation; others stress good works; still others promote reincarnation.

The other way takes the burden off humans, stating upfront people can't bridge the chasm. Instead, God must do it for them. This is the amazing message of the Bible and the foundational principle of Christianity. No other sacred book or religion proclaims this wonderful news.

Not even Mormonism.

But many people, both Christians and Mormons alike, think otherwise. They view Christianity and Mormonism as basically being the same bridge. Mormons think they have the fulness of the gospel.

In other words, they have an improved bridge. Many Christians consider Mormonism as just another flavor of Christianity.

There are various reasons for this. A significant one is that most Mormons don't have a correct understanding of Christianity. It would seem with all the information on the Internet, they would be better acquainted with it. The Internet, however, has frequently increased their confusion by exposing them to many different Christian messages.

Mormons aren't the only ones confused. Many Christians' grasp on Christianity has become increasingly weak as they too hear these different voices. In such an environment, it becomes easier for them to categorize Mormonism as a Christian religion.

This is true especially because of something already mentioned in the preface. But it bears repeating. Mormonism sounds so Christian! It uses many important biblical words like grace and salvation. But it defines them so differently. In order to see the differences between the beliefs, it is essential to know these different definitions. One of Truth in Love Ministry's most popular resources, a *Dictionary of Mormonese*, gives the definitions used by the LDS Church for these important biblical words.

In the following pages, we compare what Mormonism and Christianity say about this most important topic of crossing the chasm. It is our prayer that this study will help you share with your Mormon friends the wonderful message of how Christ bridged the chasm for them.

PART 1

HOW WIDE IS THE CHASM?

PART 1

INTRODUCTION

Before crossing a chasm, it only makes sense to determine its width. To do otherwise would be a formula for disaster. Therefore, before talking about how to cross the chasm, we need to talk about its nature and size.

At the very beginning, God crossed over the chasm. He took the initiative even though he was Adam and Eve's creator. He bridged the gap by walking and talking with Adam and Eve. But then sin shattered their idyllic relationship and substantially widened the chasm.

So how wide is it?

Mormonism and the Bible answer this question in drastically different ways. We will explore their answers in the next two chapters.

CHAPTER 1

WHO GOD IS

Imagine a Christian and a Mormon standing at the edge of the chasm separating them from God. As they look across, each sees God quite differently. Mormons see someone who is similar to them. God is only **different in degree**. He was human but has progressed further than they have. In a very real way, Mormons view God like small children look at their parents. They believe they will grow and become like him. The classic LDS couplet, coined by one of their prophets, Lorenzo Snow, states it succinctly:

> As man is, God once was
> As God now is, man may be

LDS members sometimes claim this saying is outdated. Nonetheless, their official manuals still cite it. For example, it serves as the foundation of an entire chapter in a manual published in 2012. (*Teachings of Presidents of the Church: Lorenzo Snow* 83-91).

In striking contrast, the Bible describes God as a completely different being. He is unique in every sense of the word. There is no other being like him. He is in a class all by himself. "I am God, and there is no other" (Isaiah 45:22). He is completely different, not only from humans, but also from spiritual creatures like angels. **He is different in his very essence.**

> MORMONISM: GOD IS DIFFERENT **IN DEGREE**
>
> BIBLE: GOD IS DIFFERENT **IN ESSENCE**

These two understandings of God result in drastically different views of the width of the chasm. *Mormonism's concept of a God similar to us narrows the chasm. The biblical teaching of a God completely different from us widens the chasm.*

Accurately seeing its width is the essential first step in crossing the chasm. This chapter gauges its width by taking a closer look at who God is. Chapter Two looks at who humans are. Together they show how incredibly wide the chasm truly is. They also show how Mormonism narrows the chasm. This tragically leads people into thinking they must, with a little help from God, bridge the chasm themselves.

MORMONISM'S VIEW OF GOD

Human in Nature and Relationships

As already mentioned, the LDS God is very human. In fact, the predominant aspect emphasized in Mormonism is God's human body. "His eternal spirit is housed in a tangible body of flesh and bones (see D&C 130:22)" (*Gospel Principles* 6). A physical body is often the only characteristic mentioned. They frequently refer to this teaching to prove God has revealed to their prophets the fulness of the gospel.

The fact that the LDS God has a physical body makes sense because, as quoted above, Mormonism teaches God is an exalted man. Joseph Smith taught, "God Himself was once as we are now, and is an exalted man, and sits enthroned in yonder heavens!" (*Teachings of Presidents of the Church: Joseph Smith* 40). President Henry B. Eyring simply said: "The Father and the Son are resurrected beings" ("His Spirit to Be with You" 86).

Not only does God have a human body; he also has human relationships. He has a wife. In fact, he *must* have a wife because having children is an integral aspect of being God. The following is part of a dialogue printed in one of their official teacher's guides.

> "I see. His purpose is 'to bring to pass the immortality and eternal life of man'" (Moses 1:39).
>
> "Which involves giving birth to spirit children and setting them on the road to exaltation. And if that is to be done, you must have an exalted man and …"
>
> "An exalted woman."
>
> "Exactly. An exalted man and woman who have been joined together in an eternal marriage." (*Doctrine and Covenants Instructor's Guide* Lesson 50)

Today, there is increased focus on this exalted woman whom Mormons have titled Heavenly Mother. "The doctrine of a Heavenly

Mother is a cherished and distinctive belief among Latter-day Saints" (Gospel Topics Essays, *Mother in Heaven*). Even if they don't specifically talk about her, they often speak about their heavenly parents. This is a noticeable change. Just a few years ago, they almost always referred only to Heavenly Father.

Although the emphasis on Heavenly Mother is quite recent, their emphasis on God having an eternal marriage has been around for decades. According to Mormonism, eternal or celestial marriage is essential to being God and becoming like God. The only place Mormons can enter into an *eternal* marriage is in the temple. This, then, becomes a main motivation for becoming worthy to enter the temple.

They also talk about eternal marriage regularly—even at early ages. I remember attending a sacrament meeting where an eight-year old girl emotionally testified to her dream of being married eternally. "Families Forever" remains a rallying cry for many Mormons.

This human God is who Mormons see when they look across the chasm. They rarely speak of his divine attributes like being all-knowing, all-powerful and always present. When such attributes are mentioned, they are rarely used to comfort people. In most cases, they are mentioned with no additional comments.

> Some Mormons say they aren't sure they want to live with God in heaven.

This illustrates a striking paradox. Although the LDS God is so human, he's not very personal. Many former Mormons have said how, as Mormons, they saw God as a cold and distant parent. One woman talked about how she had a view of God which inspired devotion, but still kept him at arms-length.

Even more surprising, some practicing Mormons say they aren't sure they want to live with God in heaven. They think they will be more comfortable outside of his presence!

Many Gods

The couplet quoted at the beginning of this chapter leads to the conclusion that there are many gods. That is accurate. D&C 132:19-20, for example, talks about people receiving exaltation, the LDS term for becoming a god.

> and they shall pass by the angels, and the gods, which are set there, to their exaltation and glory in all things, as hath been sealed upon their heads, which glory shall be a fulness and a continuation of the seeds forever and ever.
>
> Then shall they be gods, because they have no end; therefore shall they be from everlasting to everlasting, because they continue; then shall they be above all, because all things are subject unto them. Then shall they be gods, because they have all power, and the angels are subject unto them.

Another of their scriptures, *The Book of Abraham*, talks about the Gods creating the world. Chapters 4-5 are a reworking of Genesis 1-2. "Gods" are mentioned no less than 47 times! (As the last two paragraphs demonstrate, Mormonism sometimes uses "gods" and other times "Gods." They usually capitalize it when talking about those who have become gods while using the lower case to refer to those who can attain it in the future. Even in this there is no consistency as, sometimes, it deviates from this pattern.)

Despite these and other references, many Mormons don't focus on their many gods. But it does bother some. Gina described her experience: "I started thinking about who God is to me. Is he really just one in a billion other potential gods?" NO that could not be true. . . I raised these questions with my husband, who looked at me as though I had gone crazy."

Mormonism's doctrine of many gods can become another element blurring the way Mormons see God. Even though he is so much like them, he is indistinct and impersonal to many.

THE BIBLE'S VIEW OF GOD

The biblical view of God is so different! Here, too, we encounter a paradox. Even though he is so different, we don't see him as distant but as caring and loving. We enjoy a personal and intimate relationship with him even though he is far greater than us.

As already stated, the Bible describes God as unique. It repeatedly states there is only one God. Then it blows our minds by describing three distinct persons (Father, Son, and Holy Spirit) individually as God. Without using the term, the Bible identifies God as triune: one being consisting of three distinct and separate persons. God is so different that we can't wrap our minds around his awesome nature.

Surprisingly, God's triune nature is not what the Bible highlights. It talks much more about his divine attributes. It speaks of his justice and how sin must be punished. It warns about his devastating eternal punishment for all who aren't covered with Christ's perfection through faith.

What it emphasizes, however, is his desire to save all people. "This is good, and pleases God our Savior, who wants all people to be saved and to come to a knowledge of the truth" (1 Timothy 2:3-4). The Bible focuses on God's love. Its best-known verse, John 3:16, declares the greatness of God's love. He gave his Son for the whole world! Examples of God's love can be found on almost every page of the Bible. The apostle John summed it up: "God is love" (1 John 4:8).

God's love controls and guides everything he does. Here are three examples.

- In **Psalm 139**, David talks about several of God's awesome attributes. He cites them not because they intimidate him, but because they comfort him. Verses 8-10 are typical: "If I go up to the heavens, you are there; if I make my bed in the depths, you are there. If I rise on the wings of the dawn, if I settle on the far side of the sea, even there your hand will guide me, your right hand will hold me fast." The fact that God is everywhere gave David comfort; God would be guiding him and holding him during every moment of his life.

- **Matthew 10:29-31:** "Are not two sparrows sold for a penny? Yet not one of them will fall to the ground outside your Father's care. And even the very hairs of your head are all numbered. So don't be afraid; you are worth more than many sparrows." Jesus refers to God's omniscience to comfort his disciples.

- **Romans 8:28:** "And we know that in all things God works for the good of those who love him, who have been called according to his purpose." Because he is all-powerful and all-wise, God works good in every situation his believing children encounter.

Such examples could be multiplied many times over. Even though the Bible says God is vastly superior, he still treats people in a caring and personal way. Even though the chasm is incredibly wide, his light and love beam brightly across it.

DISCUSSING GOD WITH MORMONS

Christians often talk with Mormons about these differing views of God, especially God's triune nature and Mormonism's rejection of it. In fact, this is one of the first things many Christians want to discuss. However, for several reasons, beginning with the Trinity can be more frustrating than productive.

First, Mormonism's view of God doesn't bother most Mormons. In fact, many prefer it to the biblical view. We have asked many converts to the LDS Church what first attracted them to it. We were surprised by their answers. We thought they would point to Mormonism's emphasis on the family or their morality. Many did, but the number one reason was Mormonism made God understandable. Many talked about how, as a Christian, they struggled with the teaching of the Trinity.

Secondly, discussing God's nature is an intellectual subject. Over a century ago, the respected Christian historian, Philip Schaff, said that unbelievers "are seldom convinced by argument, for the springs of unbelief are in the heart rather than in the head" (5). This is what we encounter to this day. In fact, we have found many Mormons like intellectual conversations. They view them as safer than talking about personal topics, such as their standing with God.

Thirdly, most Mormons have a wrong conception of the biblical teaching of the Trinity. They think the Bible doesn't keep the three persons distinct. For example, Mormons routinely ask if Jesus prayed to himself when he hung on the cross. These misconceptions make it extremely difficult to have productive conversations about God's nature.

Adding to the confusion is Mormonism's teaching that the Father, Son and Holy Ghost comprise the godhead. Their first Article of Faith states: "We believe in God, the Eternal Father, and in His Son, Jesus Christ, and in the Holy Ghost." In addition, Mormonism talks about the three persons having a oneness of purpose. This has caused some Christians to wonder if Mormonism does indeed have the correct view of God.

We have gone into some detail because we are often asked about this. We wholeheartedly agree that we will eventually need to discuss God's triune nature with them. We, however, have found Mormons to be much more receptive to such a discussion after they have seen God's great love in Jesus. Our encouragement is to talk first and thoroughly about Jesus. Once they have a relationship with him, other things fall into place.

CONCLUSION

Although Mormonism's God is like them, he comes off as distant and detached. Even though it pictures God as being close to them in his nature, its view of him is quite fuzzy. The one thing Mormons see clearly is that God is human: both in his nature and his relationships.

On the other hand, the God of the Bible is completely different from us and vastly superior to us but is highly interested and involved with us. He is warm, personal, and kind. Even though the chasm is incredibly wide, the Bible brings him into sharp focus.

> MORMONISM: GOD IS **HUMAN BUT DISTANT**
>
> BIBLE: GOD IS **UNIQUE AND PERSONAL**

The contrast between a distant human God and a caring divine God is one which is especially beneficial when talking with Mormons. Because Mormons put so much emphasis on feelings, this approach connects with them.

How wide is the chasm between God and man? Mormonism's view of God narrows it while the Bible's widens it. This pattern continues in the next chapter.

CHAPTER 2

WHO WE ARE

Imagine standing at the edge of the Grand Canyon. The views are majestic. Pictures can't capture the immense size. At its widest point, the canyon stretches for 18 miles. It yawns open at least a mile down. The panorama takes your breath away. If you're not careful, it could take you away! You are mindful not to lose your footing. The abrupt drop off is unnerving. This vast scene provides a beautiful, yet humbling perspective.

Now imagine you need to cross the canyon to live eternally with God. What was once awe-inspiring is now just awful. You are speechless in a whole new way. The very prospect is terrifying. Many simply give up and put a life with God out of their mind.

Some desperately seek a path forward. They nervously pace back and forth along the rim in search of the closest point. If they can find a narrow gap, they hope crossing it might be possible.

As mentioned in the last chapter, Mormonism attempts to narrow this distance to God. Since God resembles a man, he does not appear quite so far from them. Since they possess his potential, they do not seem so far from him. From this perspective, the gap has shrunk. Crossing the divide is not quite as intimidating as it once was.

The Bible paints a very different picture. God is infinitely greater than us. Sin greatly expanded the divide that separates us from a holy and righteous God. We don't start from a positive or even neutral position. We are in a fallen state that makes it impossible for us to cross the chasm.

The difference between the Mormon and biblical Christian perspectives is not subtle. The end results couldn't be further apart. This is important to understand as we witness to Mormons.

MORMONISM'S VIEW OF OURSELVES

A Distorted Perspective

If you go to a carnival, you can usually follow youthful laughter to the distortion mirrors in the funhouse. Curved and tilted surfaces transform your appearance. Some stretch you out to look tall and skinny. Others shrink you down to appear short and fat. As you can imagine, people gravitate toward the mirrors that are more complimentary.

The distortion mirrors of Mormonism are one of its attractions. It begins by distorting the picture of their potential. Again, this is rooted in the famous LDS couplet:

> As man is, God once was
> As God now is, man may be

Consider the far-reaching implications of that statement. If God was once a man, then it must also be possible for man to become God. The ultimate goal of Mormonism is not merely to live *with* God, but to live *as* god. "Those who inherit the highest degree of the celestial kingdom…become gods" (*Gospel Principles* 272). Many Mormons may not focus on this (or even think they can achieve it), yet the teachings and activity of Mormonism all drive toward this goal.

While this is still the teaching of the church today, it is not emphasized. Some may even be unfamiliar with it. Instead, many describe how they will become "like God." This is an ongoing process. By keeping the commandments and walking along the covenant path, they hope to step closer toward that goal each day.

> The ultimate goal of Mormonism is not merely to live *with* God, but to live *as* god.

On the surface, becoming a god would seem impossible. Mormonism answers this discouragement by distorting not just their potential but also the timeline. It teaches all people originated in a preexistence. There progression already began. The fact anyone comes to earth and has a body is proof they used agency (freedom to make choices) wisely. The conditions into which they were born might be further evidence of their obedience as a noble and valiant spirit. Blessings they now experience may be traced back to following Heavenly Father's will and proving their worthiness before they were ever born.

Even if they don't get everything correct now, Mormonism teaches they will have more time in a spirit world after this life. "[Those in the spirit world] are striving with all their might—laboring and toiling diligently as any individual would to accomplish an act in this world" (*Teachings of Presidents of the Church: Brigham Young* 281). Twisting the timeline leads many to believe they are already well on their way toward godhood.

Mormonism also distorts their nature. It teaches people are the spirit children of Heavenly Father and Heavenly Mother. "We were His children before we came to this world, and we will be His children forevermore. This basic truth should change the way we look at ourselves" ("Four Titles" 58). As literal children of God, they have divine potential. Their goal is to unlock this potential.

Another distortion is the view that people are born good. Their purpose is to develop godlike qualities. All people can "progress toward perfection and ultimately realize their divine destiny" (The Family: A Proclamation to the World). They do this through a time of testing here on earth. Resisting temptation demonstrates devotion to God and is evidence of their progression to be more like him. The implication is they have the ability to keep all the commandments. In fact, LDS scriptures teach God wouldn't give a commandment they couldn't keep: "I know that the Lord giveth no commandments unto the children of men, save he shall prepare a way for them that they may accomplish the thing which he commandeth them" (1 Nephi 3:7).

Wendy Nelson, wife of LDS President Russell Nelson, wrote the children's book *The Not Even Once Club*. It describes itself as "an adorable and appealing way to engage children in a story that will help them choose for themselves to keep the commandments and to never break them. Not even once." The premise is if they try

> **MORMONISM**
> The premise is that if they try hard enough it is possible to be perfect.

hard enough, it is possible to be perfect.

This distorted view of their potential, their timeline and their nature has the unintended consequence of placing constant pressure on Mormons. God is not only cold and impersonal as noted in chapter 1, he can be compared to a demanding parent. All parents want their children to develop their gifts and encourage them along the way. Some, however, while well-intentioned, push their children in athletics and the arts to the brink of breaking. "Just try harder" and "don't stop trying" can lead to a belief that acceptance is based on performance. When they fail, it can lead to despair. Imagine how much more of a burden they feel when the impossible expectations are set by their Heavenly Father.

Hayley grew up in Mormonism. She struggled from little on. She says, "I knew I was not good enough. I knew it was impossible to live up to God's standard, and I was in despair." She never felt worthy. Filled with fear and shame, she was sure she was going to hell. Hayley is not alone. Many Mormons have privately shared their struggle with us. They're pressured to be perfect. When they inevitably fall short, they feel like a failure.

Mormonism Minimizes Sin

Mormonism not only raises their potential. It also lowers God's expectations by minimizing sin. This may come as a surprise to some because there is such an emphasis on moral behavior and family values. They are focused on keeping the commandments. Their piety extends to avoiding tobacco, alcohol, and coffee (D&C 89). All of these additional rules might lead one to believe Mormonism raises up the law.

In reality, it actually lowers the bar to make God's law achievable. It teaches "sin is *knowingly choosing to do* wrong or not to do right" (*Plan of Salvation* 9, emphasis added). Many believe an evil thought is not wrong; it only becomes wrong when acted upon. It speaks more often of mistakes or missteps. Further, they are taught children are not able to sin until age 8 (D&C 29:46-47). Even when sin is acknowledged, there is more focus on its earthly consequences and the harm it brings to a person's progression than on its eternal consequences.

Downplaying sin starts with the very first one. Mormonism presents an upside-down view of the fall. They are taught following Satan's temptation in Eden was a courageous, positive step. "Latter-day revelation makes clear that the Fall is a blessing" (*Preach My Gospel* 59). It teaches this first sin made it possible for mankind to obtain physical bodies, overcome temptation and progress along God's plan.

Furthermore, Mormonism confuses God's commands in the Bible. In the Old Testament, God established civil laws to govern Israel as a nation and ceremonial laws to oversee their religious practices. God also established the moral law, the Ten Commandments, which are reaffirmed in the New Testament. Unfortunately, Mormons are taught most references to the law in the New Testament point back to Old Testament laws that no longer apply today.

CROSSING THE CHASM IS:

MORMONISM: PROGRESSION TOWARD THEIR POTENTIAL

BIBLE: DESTINATION WITH THE DIVINE

In practice, Mormons are offered frequent encouragements: "just keep improving" or "God only asks you to do your best." The result of lowering God's standards leads some Mormons to believe they rarely, if ever, sin. Some ex-Mormons we've encountered describe how they weren't discouraged because they didn't believe they had sin.

When their ability is raised and God's law is lowered, it gives them a more positive view of themselves. Keeping the commandments now seems possible. Crossing the chasm within Mormonism is more about progression toward their potential than a destination with the divine. This emphasis does not draw them closer to God. Many Mormons describe how distant God still seems. Deep down, all is not well in their relationship with God.

THE BIBLE'S VIEW OF OURSELVES

Perfect in the Beginning

In order to honestly deal with a problem, you must first have a realistic picture of it. The distortion mirrors in Mormonism may provide a complimentary reflection, but they don't prepare a person to cross the chasm. Instead, we need to see ourselves through the same lens God sees us. This is why it's necessary to turn to his law: "Therefore no one will be declared righteous in God's sight by the works of the law; rather, through the law we become conscious of our sin" (Romans 3:20). The law wasn't given to pat ourselves on the back at how good we are. God's law is a mirror and provides a clear reflection of just how far we have fallen.

Our first parents, Adam and Eve, trace their origin to Eden. Where Mormonism's preexistence asserts some spirits were already becoming better than others, the biblical record speaks of perfection. God created both and personally breathed life into them. They were a smashing success in his eyes according to his perfect design.

Adam and Eve experienced a loving, personal relationship with their Creator. They were made in the image of God. Where Mormonism describes a physical image, the Bible emphasizes a spiritual image (Ephesians 4:24, Colossians 3:10). They were righteous and holy. They wanted what God wanted. They were able to approach God and enjoy his companionship. They walked and talked in his presence. They were the crown of creation and the apple of his eye. There was no need for progression; they were already at the top.

Even though they experienced a close relationship, their difference in essence from God was clear. The Creator uniquely gifted his creatures for service. They were made to bring him glory.

God provided a unique way for them to show their thanks. He created a tree from which they were not to eat. It was a place of worship where they could exercise their free will and demonstrate their love for God. By choosing good over evil and God over themselves, they could continue to enjoy this relationship with him.

Tragically, it didn't last.

The Chasm is Widened

Satan tempted them with the idea they could be like God (Genesis 3:5). They fell for it and all creation fell with them. Shockwaves resonated throughout the earth. The chasm between God and mankind widened dramatically. God's perfect image in them was shattered. The Bible clearly emphasizes a downward fall: "Just as sin entered the world through one man, and death through sin, and in this way death came to all people, because all sinned" (Romans 5:12).

Adam and Eve now found themselves on the opposite side of God looking across an impassible divide. Satan's lie that they would become like God echoed hollow down the chasm. When the dust settled, God was impossibly far away. They felt alone. They now experienced shame and fear. They turned on each other.

The days of walking with God and being perfectly in sync with his will have been replaced by a sinful mind hostile to God (Romans 8:7). A far cry from being good by nature, their children inherited the sin of Adam and a predisposition toward evil.

It's common for people today to hope God, out of love, will just sweep sin under the rug. This asks God to be tolerant of some evil. Most don't realize such a perspective essentially asks a holy God to be evil. Others hope it will all work out if they do more good than bad. Yet even their best efforts are filthy rags (Isaiah 64:6) and an insult to God. A just God can't look the other way. Sin is so serious the Bible describes us as objects of his wrath (Ephesians 2:3).

While this biblical dose of reality may be difficult to acknowledge, it is essential toward understanding the distance of the divide. When we recognize we cannot possibly bridge the gap, we can do nothing but fall to our knees before his mercy. It's there we discover his love shines brightest.

Sharing the Law

Many Christians are eager to share the gospel with Mormon family and friends. Sharing good news is easy. If you and your spouse are expecting a child, you look forward to telling others. If a loved one has passed, it may be more difficult news to share. But refusing to share important, yet difficult news is unloving.

Imagine you're struggling with pain so you go to your doctor. After a series of tests, the doctor discovers every part of your body is riddled with cancer. Is it loving for your doctor not to share that news? Of course not! It's part of his job. So it is also with witnessing. We need to share the message that we have all been thoroughly infected by sin. We can witness with confidence because we also know the cure.

> **WITNESSING TIP**
>
> SHARE THE SERIOUSNESS, EXTENT AND PENALTY OF SIN.

As we share the law, it is critical to show the *seriousness* of sin. Moses, for example, led the stubborn people of Israel through the wilderness for 40 years. God had revealed spectacular signs through him. Moses had done incredible good. Yet, in a moment of frustration, he struck a rock instead of speaking to it (Numbers 20:1-12). Most would consider it a minor offense. Yet God didn't weigh his good against his bad any more than a judge today would suspend a prison sentence because the accused was known for doing some good. God looks at our entire record. This single instance prevented Moses from entering the Promised Land. It only takes one pinprick to pop a balloon. "Whoever keeps the whole law and yet stumbles at just one point is guilty of breaking all of it" (James 2:10). Just one offense brings the punishment for every law in the book.

We also need to describe the *extent* of sin. We have not simply sinned once, but we have a countless record of offenses against God.

This is important to emphasize because some Mormons may believe they have kept all the commandments like the Pharisees in the New Testament. The Bible teaches anyone who hates is a murderer (1 John 3:15) and anyone who looks with lust is an adulterer (Matthew 5:28). If we worry, we add fear to concern and sin by not trusting in God. It's important to help Mormons discover how often we all sin.

As we share the law, it is helpful to take a non-confrontational approach. The law is a message that can unintentionally create defensive barriers. If you are authentic about your own struggles, (for example, with worry or a lack of contentment), you're not only being vulnerable and showing you're no better than they are, but you're also inviting them to open their heart and share struggles of their own. This approach can be liberating for those in a culture where the pressure is on to show how good they're doing.

Finally, lay out the *penalty* for sin. "The wages of sin is death" (Romans 6:23). This is not just physical death, but spiritual, eternal death. Mormons are taught most people will go to one level of heaven or another. It's vital for them to understand sin is so serious that God's punishment is outer darkness (the Mormon understanding of hell). Be prepared for many to be surprised because they will be hearing this for the first time.

Sarah was reaching out to Mormon sister missionaries. They grew very close. Finally, through tears, she laid it on the line. "Girls, I'm concerned you're following a false gospel that can't save you and will lead to eternity without Christ." This witness was followed by a heartfelt

> "You're the first who pleaded with me not to go [to hell]. That is the most loving thing I've ever heard."

response: "I've had Christian friends tell me I was going to hell. You're the first who pleaded with me not to go there. That is the most loving thing I've ever heard."

Sharing the law doesn't have to be hard. Hayley told us, "Even though we were taught everyone would go to one level of heaven or another, deep down, I was sure I was going to hell." Many are afraid they're not good enough. Sarah was relieved to hear of her sin because it took the pressure off: "I now celebrate my nothingness." When we help Mormons see themselves as the Bible describes, they will better understand those feelings and be positioned for God's solution.

Reality Brings Relief

Go back to the picture of trying to cross the Grand Canyon. It's a terrifying prospect. Many desperately search for a narrow point, hoping that it may be achievable.

Mormonism presents that perspective. It lowers the view of God. At the same time, it raises a view of self. By bringing God closer to them (chapter 1) and them closer to God (chapter 2), it would appear to narrow the gap. The irony is it does just the opposite. Those who try to cross the chasm on their own describe God as further away than ever.

> **MORMONISM:** NARROW CHASM, YET GOD IS DISTANT
>
> **BIBLE:** EXPANSIVE CHASM, YET GOD IS NEAR

Biblical Christianity reveals an accurate picture of the chasm. God is sovereign and holy. Our sin is evidence of how far we've fallen.

The gap to God is so great we would never even consider trying to build our own bridge. In spite of this, God doesn't seem distant at all. "The LORD is near to all who call on him…he hears their cry and saves them" (Psalm 145:18-19). The only way to cross the chasm is for God in his love to build the bridge for us. So that's what he did.

PART 2

HOW TO CROSS THE CHASM

PART 2

INTRODUCTION

Crossing the chasm will require a bridge. The distance is great. The destination is life with God. This can be no ordinary bridge.

The most common bridge design to span a chasm is an arch bridge. This evenly distributes support to both sides. Typical construction involves building a portion from each side and then meeting in the middle. This is neither the biblical nor the Mormon model.

The Mormon model comes with blueprints from Heavenly Father. Unfortunately, his plans call for construction that depends mainly on them. Imagine trying to build a bridge where the weight falls on you. This is a flawed plan from the start. Even though it's destined to collapse on itself eventually, you're told not to ask questions or worry about it. So, you begin laying out thin, brittle boards of your own works. They're cracked and decaying, yet you're urged just to keep

busy building, and everything will work out.

Occasionally you look down with terror. In those moments, you're faced with a choice. Some continue building, figuring they've gone this far, and they can't give up now. Others look back and consider getting off the bridge while they still can. Tragically, some give up in despair and jump off.

The biblical model employs an architectural design unlike any other. The Father's love moved him to plan for a bridge that wouldn't fail. To achieve this, it couldn't rely on us. Instead, it is supported by God alone.

Jesus, the Son, constructed the bridge to our side of the chasm. He followed the Father's plan without fail. His flawless life assembled the perfect platform. Jesus, our substitute, built a sturdy and reliable bridge upon which we can count.

God knew designing and building the bridge wasn't enough. It only serves its ultimate purpose if people use it. So, the Spirit goes to work in our hearts. When we give up on our own bridge and trust in Christ alone, the Spirit places us on God's bridge. Safe and secure, we can now cross the chasm.

CHAPTER 3

THE FATHER'S PLAN

World-class architects have designed some of the most famous bridges. A perfect architect planned the bridge crossing the chasm between God and humanity. Both the Bible and Mormonism identify that architect as God the Father. They both speak of his plan for reconciling God and mankind.

But the plans are vastly different. In the Bible, God builds the bridge from his side of the chasm and only relies on divine effort. He knows that humanity is worthless (Romans 3:12) because of sin's devastation. Mankind can't give even the slightest support to the bridge. Therefore, he planned the bridge to be built entirely by Jesus.

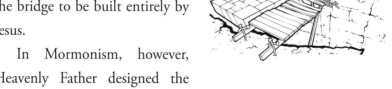

In Mormonism, however, Heavenly Father designed the bridge to be supported on both sides of the chasm. And he didn't equally distribute the weight. In his plan, humanity bears the vast majority of the bridge's weight.

This is a crucial fact but one not easily seen. At first glance, the bridges appear quite similar. Some even think they are identical. A significant reason for the confusion is that the Bible and Mormonism use many of the same words to describe the bridges. They, however, define these terms in drastically different ways. We will point out examples as we go along.

In the coming chapters, we will examine both bridges. The closer we look, the clearer we will see how dissimilar they truly are.

MORMONISM'S PLAN OF SALVATION

Humanity's Huge Role

It's difficult to overemphasize the role the plan of salvation plays in Mormonism. It's cited at every turn and is truly foundational.

Similarly, it's difficult to overemphasize the role humanity plays in the plan. President Dieter F. Uchtdorf, in a General Conference talk, put it this way:

> No one else is responsible for your personal journey. The Savior will help you and prepare the way before you, but the commitment to follow Him and keep His commandments must come from you. That is your sole burden, your sole privilege. ("A Yearning for Home" 24)

Another apostle, at another General Conference, quoting D&C 93:1, said:

> The Lord has said, "Every soul who forsaketh his sins and cometh unto me, and calleth on my name, and obeyeth my voice, and keepeth my commandments, shall see my face and know that I am." *That is perhaps His ultimate promise.* (Rasband 53, emphasis added)

God's ultimate promise is conditioned on what a person does! Only after they have forsaken sin and kept the commandments will they see the Lord's face. The following quote from their manual for new members shows how far they take it.

> Complete honesty is necessary for our salvation. President Brigham Young said, "If we accept salvation on the terms it is offered to us, we have got to be honest in every thought, in our reflections, in our meditations, in our private circles, in our deals, in our declarations, and in every act of our lives" (*Teachings of Presidents of the Church: Brigham Young* [1997], 293). (*Gospel Principles* 179)

This is Mormonism 101. God doesn't *proactively* save. Rather he *reacts* to people's obedience. Its 3rd Article of Faith states: "We believe that through the Atonement of Christ, all mankind may be saved by obedience to the laws and ordinances of the Gospel." One of the most quoted verses from the Book of Mormon states: "for we know that it is by grace we are saved, after all we can do" (2 Nephi 25:23). A popular LDS manual comments on this verse: "The phrase 'after all we can do' teaches that *effort is required on our part* to receive the fulness of the Lord's grace and be made worthy to dwell with

Him (*True to the Faith* 77, emphasis added).

These quotes illustrate an important point. Mormonism does mention Jesus' atonement and God's grace. We will take a closer look at this in the next chapter. Suffice it here to say that Mormonism teaches the atonement made forgiveness *possible*. But only if a person is obedient and keeps the commandments.

> **MORMONISM**
> God doesn't *proactively* save. Rather he *reacts* to people's obedience.

Process this for a moment. Do you see how it has a small view of the Father? He doesn't help us proactively. He *only* helps us if we first qualify for it by doing all we can.

Look again at 2 Nephi 25:23. God gives grace only "after all we can do." To understand the severity of this statement, we need to know Mormonism's definition of grace. It's not the same as the Bible's definition: the incredible, undeserved love *God shows* humanity. Rather Mormonism describes it as "an enabling power" *God gives* people. Employing this definition, 2 Nephi 25:23 doesn't say God will take over for us after all we can do. Rather he will infuse us with power so we can keep on doing!

Because Mormonism does mention grace and Christ's atonement, LDS members usually fume when Christians describe Mormonism as a works-religion. Instead, refer to it as a grace plus religion. Most Mormons will accept this label. Then you can have a productive conversation on how any and all works ruin grace "And if by grace, then is it no more of works: otherwise grace is no more grace" (Romans 11:6, KJV). When it comes to salvation, God's grace and human work are mutually exclusive.

Eternal Progression

There is much more evidence of Mormonism's emphasis on human effort. For example, eternal progression is a prominent LDS doctrine. "It is important to recognize that God's ultimate purpose is our progress" (Christofferson 32). The foremost thing people must do is to continually get better.

> Like a loving parent, He merely wants you to *keep intentionally trying.* Discipleship is like learning to play the piano. Perhaps all you can do at first is play a barely recognizable rendition of "Chopsticks." But if you continue practicing, the simple tunes will one day give way to wondrous sonatas, rhapsodies, and concertos.
>
> Now, that day may not come during this life, but it will come. All God asks is that you consciously *keep striving.* ("Your Great Adventure" 88, emphasis added)

Not only does the Father want them to keep on trying. He "is constantly trying to help us become the person He knows we can become" (Held 32).

In this connection, Mormonism interprets Jesus' command to *be* perfect (Matthew 5:48) as to *become* perfect. A clear example is a Conference talk entitled, "Be Ye Therefore Perfect—Eventually." In it, an LDS apostle stated, "If we persevere, then somewhere in eternity our refinement will be finished and complete" (Holland 40).

But this isn't how they always talk. In their multi-year project of reviewing the teachings of the presidents of their church, we read this: "We are commanded to be supermen. Said the Lord, 'Be ye therefore perfect, even as your Father which is in heaven is perfect.' (Matt. 5:48.) We are gods in embryo, and the Lord demands perfection of us" (*Teachings of Presidents of the Church: Spencer W. Kimball* 96).

In this same manual, we also read about their purpose for being on earth. "We were to eliminate sins of omission and commission, and to follow the laws and commandments given us by our Father" (Ibid 3).

This focus on continually striving until the goal is achieved sometime in eternity crushes many LDS members. Sue shared how growing up she knew she wasn't good enough. She felt this way even though she tried her best to keep all the commandments. In her words, she was a "goody, goody." She finally resigned herself to the thought that, despite all she did, she was going to hell.

Lori talked about how she went to bed each night thinking she would do better the next day. This continued for 23 years. She never knew if she was loved by God or forgiven by him. But she kept on trying to improve herself. Still another woman talked about how she saw God as a demanding parent. She never felt as if she had done enough to gain his approval.

We have heard hundreds of such stories over the years. Just the fact that so many LDS members have these struggles is convincing proof that Mormonism's plan of salvation differs drastically from the biblical plan. This becomes all the clearer when we see the relief and joy they experience after learning that Jesus did everything for them.

Another striking confirmation of the bridges being different are the common LDS responses to the message of salvation by grace alone. Mormons often respond by saying that, if Jesus did it all, people could sin all they want. Or, they describe the Mormons who became Christian as "taking the easy way out." These responses alone prove that Christ-centered salvation is contrary to the message they hear in their churches.

No Undeserved Blessings

There are many other proofs showing how Mormonism's plan of salvation is built almost entirely on human effort. We point to just two more. We single these out because they are frequently cited and thus burden many LDS members.

The first is that there are no undeserved blessings in Mormonism. They often cite D&C 130:20-21. "There is a law, irrevocably decreed in heaven before the foundation of this world, upon which all blessings are predicated—And when we obtain any blessing from God, it is by obedience to that law upon which it is predicated." All blessings are predicated on, that is, they depend on, obeying the law. This is sometimes reinforced with D&C 82:10 where they believe the Lord says, "when ye do not what I say, ye have no promise."

They sometimes try to weaken this by employing verbal gymnastics. For example, after quoting D&C 130:20-21, one of their apostles stated: "That being said, you do not earn a blessing—that notion is false—but you do have to qualify for it" (Renlund 71). He then goes on to talk about how small acts of faith, which are not insignificant, are required to ignite God's promises. "Often, the activation energy needed for blessings requires more than just looking or asking; ongoing, repeated, faith-filled actions are required" (Ibid 71). Their Bible Dictionary simply states, "Blessings require some work or effort on our part before we can obtain them" (753).

Such explanations don't lessen the burden for many Mormons. They often make them feel worse!

Imagine hearing this from childhood. (One former Mormon said her father always quoted D&C 130:20-21 to her.) And then you start having problems. You immediately think these problems result from your disobedience. But nothing is obvious. You evaluate everything you have done, searching for the reason why God isn't blessing you. If the problems continue or even worsen, you increasingly despair. This is what many Mormons experience.

Bilateral Covenants

Another way Mormonism puts the stress on human activity is how it talks about covenants. Covenants play a major role in Mormonism. LDS members make covenants at their baptisms and remember them each week when they take the sacrament. They go to the temple to make more covenants. Staying on the "covenant path" is becoming an increasingly popular phrase.

> "If" is one of the biggest words in Mormonism.

Every covenant in Mormonism is bilateral, two-way. In other words, God promises to do something, but only *if* they do something first. One of their hymns says,

> Dearest children, God is near you
> Watching o'er you day and night
> And delights to own and bless you,
> *If you strive to do what's right.*
> He will bless you, He will bless you,

If you put your trust in him.
(Hymn 96, emphasis added)

"If" is one of the biggest words in Mormonism. Wherever you turn, it's there. Absolutely everything depends on what they do. As their current prophet said: "Eventual exaltation requires our complete fidelity now to covenants we make and ordinances we receive in the house of the Lord" ("Let Us All Press On" 119).

No matter from what angle you view Mormonism's plan of salvation, humans stand in the foreground while Jesus fades into the background. This is drastically different from what the Bible says. We now turn to the biblical plan.

THE BIBLE'S PLAN

As stated in the beginning of this chapter, God the Father's plan relies solely on divine efforts. He gave his Son as a sacrifice. The Son kept all the commandments for all people. He then paid the full price for all their sins. He is the only one who constructed the bridge over the chasm.

We weren't even able to find the bridge that Jesus constructed! The Holy Spirit must make people aware of it. Not only that. He also must put them on the bridge.

In the following two chapters, we will take an in-depth look at this. In the next chapter, we will study the Son's role. In Chapter Five, we will look at the Spirit's work. Here we touch only on the Father's motivation and plan.

God's Grace

The Father's *sole* motivation for bridging the chasm was his incredible love for us. "For God so loved the world that he gave his one and only Son, that whoever believes in him shall not perish but have eternal life" (John 3:16). "But because of his great love for us, God, who is rich in mercy, made us alive with Christ even when we were dead in transgressions—it is by grace you have been saved" (Ephesians 2:4-5).

As Romans 11:6 cited above clearly shows, God's grace cancels out human effort. This is the Bible's consistent message. "He has saved us and called us to a holy life—not because of anything we have done but because of his own purpose and grace" (2 Timothy 1:9). "For it is by grace you have been saved, through faith—and this is not from yourselves, it is the gift of God—not by works, so that no one can boast" (Ephesians 2:8-9).

We sometimes illustrate the destruction of adding works to grace by talking about a man being given an art masterpiece, a Rembrandt. He is overjoyed but thinks he can improve it, so he paints a flower on one corner. What has he just done? He has ruined it. Likewise, adding even the smallest work to God's masterpiece of salvation ruins it.

Sin had made the mass of humanity worthless (Romans 3:12). God not only has to do everything, but his grace is entirely undeserved. "Grace isn't just getting something we don't deserve; grace is getting the very *opposite* of what we deserve" (Braun 97).

Since his sole motivation to save us is his love, it is not affected by anything we do. Rather, "we love because he first loved us" (1 John 4:19). Philip Yancey, in his book *What's So Amazing About Grace*, puts it this way: "God loves people because of who God is, not because of who we are" (67). He also makes this comforting observation. "Grace means there is nothing we can do to make God love us more. . . grace means there is nothing we can do to make God love us less" (70).

Closely connected is the fact that God took the initiative to save us. After their fall into sin, God immediately sought out Adam and Eve. And he didn't leave them hanging. Yes, he did spell out the consequences of their sin. But he didn't put them on probation or tell them they needed to become worthy to qualify for salvation. He immediately and unconditionally promised them a son who would crush Satan's head (Genesis 3:15).

> God loves people because of who God is, not because of who we are.

God always acts proactively to save us.

> You see, at just the right time, when we were still powerless, Christ died for the ungodly. Very rarely will anyone die for a righteous person, though for a good person someone might possibly dare to die. But God demonstrates his own love for us in this: While we were still sinners, Christ died for us. (Romans 5:6-8)

Furthermore, God's love is abundant. "Where sin increased, grace increased all the more" (Romans 5:20). His grace will never run out. It will never be depleted. It is a vast, endless ocean of love. For all these reasons and more, God's grace truly deserves to be called amazing.

Since Mormonism defines grace as a power God gives people, it's important to note that the Bible occasionally uses it to describe gifts given to people. (1 Peter 4:10: "Each of you should use whatever gift you have received to serve others, as faithful stewards of God's grace in its various forms.") However, the Bible never uses it this way *in the context of salvation*. When the topic is how we are saved, grace is always synonymous with God's love.

When their eyes are opened to biblical grace, Mormons are profoundly affected. Lori, quoted above, also said: "There are not enough words to describe what it is like to be living in the light and love of Jesus, to be secure with him." Another said: "I was liberated, and I felt like I could relax and be at peace with myself. In the LDS church, I always felt that grace was completely conditional."

Unilateral Covenant

MORMONISM: BILATERAL COVENANT
BIBLE: UNILATERAL COVENANT

Like Mormonism, the Bible also talks about covenants. And sometimes, like the covenant established on Mt. Sinai, they are two-sided, bilateral. Unlike covenants in Mormonism, however, the covenant which spells out God's plan of salvation is *unilateral*, one-sided. It's all about what God will do.

We see this in the Garden of Eden when God immediately promised a Savior. His promise wasn't conditioned on anything Adam or Eve or their descendants had to do. God would do it. Period. Its unilateral nature comes out very clearly in Jeremiah 31:31-34. As you read these passages, note the total absence of the word "if." Note how

God does the work while humans are entirely on the receiving end.

> "The days are coming," declares the LORD,
>   "when I will make a new covenant
> with the people of Israel
>   and with the people of Judah.
> It will not be like the covenant
>   I made with their ancestors
> when I took them by the hand
>   to lead them out of Egypt,
> because they broke my covenant,
>   though I was a husband to them,"
> declares the LORD.
> "This is the covenant I will make with the people of Israel
>   after that time," declares the LORD.
> "I will put my law in their minds
>   and write it on their hearts.
> I will be their God,
>   and they will be my people.
> No longer will they teach their neighbor,
>   or say to one another, 'Know the LORD,'
> because they will all know me,
>   from the least of them to the greatest,"
> declares the LORD.
> "For I will forgive their wickedness
>   and will remember their sins no more."

"I will forgive their wickedness." Period. The biblical plan of salvation begins and ends with God doing everything for us. It is a *unilateral* activity.

Romans 6:23 sums up the contributions of God and mankind. "For the wages of sin is death, but the gift of God is eternal life in Christ Jesus our Lord." Death is what we *earned*. It is what we deserved. But what we receive as a *gift* is eternal life. We receive it "in Christ Jesus our Lord." We now turn to his all-important role in bridging the chasm.

CHAPTER 4

THE SON'S ROLE

At first glance, it looks like the role Jesus plays in salvation is similar in Mormonism and the Bible. Both refer to him as the Son of God. Both call him Savior. Both talk about his atonement to pay for our sins.

But the similarities are only surface deep. The more a person studies the Bible and then Mormonism, the more one sees how differently each describes Christ's role.

MORMONISM'S VIEW

Who Jesus Is

We begin by looking at who Mormonism says Jesus is. "Our Savior is the Firstborn in the spirit, the Only Begotten in the flesh" (*Teachings of Presidents of the Church: Joseph Fielding Smith* 52). But what does this mean?

First, consider the phrase "Firstborn in the spirit." Here's the explanation. "Among the spirit children of Elohim, the first-born was and is Jehovah, or Jesus Christ, to whom all others are juniors" (*Teachings of Presidents of the Church: Joseph F. Smith* 355). In other words, Jesus is not eternal or equal with the Father. Instead, he is the Father's literal spirit child. Since Mormonism teaches that all people are also spirit children, this means Jesus is our brother, even before he came to earth.

As the quote further shows, Mormonism identifies God the Father as Elohim and Jesus as Jehovah. It does this even though the Bible sometimes uses both names as a joint title for God ("LORD God" in most Bible translations).

Similarly, it redefines the title "Only Begotten." "Jesus is the only person on earth to be born of a mortal mother and an immortal Father. That is why He is called the Only Begotten Son" (*Gospel Principles* 53). In other words, Mormonism teaches that the Father *physically* fathered Jesus in the flesh.

Although Jesus' divinity is an important topic, it usually is not a topic which results in productive witnessing conversations. Most LDS members aren't bothered by Mormonism's view of Jesus. Thus, they often respond with a shrug and quickly disengage.

What Jesus Did – The Atonement

It is much more productive to discuss what Jesus did for us. If Mormonism's view of Jesus is confusing, the waters become even murkier when we look at how it describes what Jesus did for us. The most common term it uses is the atonement. (It rarely uses other biblical words like justification or redemption.) Therefore, we need to take a close look at how Mormonism defines atonement.

CHAPTER 4: THE SON'S ROLE

"Jesus's atoning sacrifice took place in the Garden of Gethsemane and on the cross at Calvary" (*True to the Faith* 17). This represents a slight shift in emphasis from previous years. Not so long ago, Mormons almost exclusively pointed to Jesus' bloody sweat in the Garden of Gethsemane as his atoning sacrifice for us. Rarely did they mention his crucifixion. While they now include both, their focus remains on Gethsemane.

Sometimes Christians want to focus the discussion on the importance Mormonism places on Jesus' suffering in Gethsemane. But such a discussion is majoring in minors. Focusing on what Mormonism says the atonement *accomplished* is much more crucial.

The following quote is representative. "The great sacrifice He made to pay for our sins and overcome death is called the Atonement" (*Gospel Principles* 59). It sounds so good! But as we delve deeper, this initial good impression wanes.

Not much needs to be said about their belief that Jesus overcame death for mankind. That Jesus rose from the dead and therefore, we will also, is something with which we agree.

> **MORMONISM**
> All mankind may be saved by obedience to the laws and ordinances of the Gospel.

The other aspect, that he paid for our sins, needs a much closer look. Mormonism states: "Although all people will be resurrected only those who accept the Atonement will be saved from spiritual death" (*Gospel Principles* 62). It then references their Third Article of Faith. "We believe that through the Atonement of Christ, all mankind may be saved, by obedience to the laws and ordinances of the Gospel."

The phrase "by obedience to the laws and ordinances of the Gospel" stops us in our tracks. Their manual for missionary service explains it this way: "Heavenly Father has provided us, His children, with a way to be successful in this life and to return to live in His presence. However, we must be pure and clean through obedience in order to do so" (*Preach My Gospel* 31).

Here is how it was explained in a General Conference talk.

> We stand all amazed at the Savior's grace in giving us second chances in overcoming sin, or failures of the heart.
>
> No one is more on our side than the Savior. He allows us to take and keep retaking His exams. To become like Him will require countless *second chances* in our day-to-day struggles with the natural man … If to err is human nature, how many failures will it take us until our nature is no longer human but divine? Thousands? More likely a million.
>
> …the Savior paid an infinite price to give us as many chances as it would take to successfully pass our mortal probation. (Robbins 22)

Jesus gave them second, third, a million chances. But they must pass the exam. In fact, the struggle to "overcome sin" continues after death. Talking about the dead, D&C 138:59 states: "And after they have paid the penalty of their transgressions, and are washed clean, shall receive a reward according to their works, for they are heirs of salvation." This is not an obscure reference either. It was quoted by a member of the First Presidency at the October 2019 General

Conference (Oaks 29).

LDS salvation is always conditioned on a person's obedience to the laws of the Gospel. Jesus gives people many chances to overcome sin. The dead must still pay the penalty for their transgressions. It's obvious their concept of Jesus as Savior bears little resemblance to biblical teaching.

Still today, the clearest explanation of how they see Jesus as their Savior is a parable told by Boyd K. Packer, a prominent LDS apostle. Although he first told it in 1977, it is still used today. For example, it is quoted in the chapter on the Atonement in *Gospel Principles*, their basic manual for new members (63-65).

It pictures God the Father as a creditor and a man as a debtor. The day came when the contract fell due. The creditor demanded full payment. The debtor couldn't pay so he begged for mercy. The creditor says mercy is one-sided; justice must also be served. Then the debtor's friend steps in to mediate. He asks the creditor if he would free the debtor of his obligation on the condition that he would pay his friend's entire debt. The creditor agrees. Then the mediator turns to the debtor.

> "If I pay your debt, will you accept me as your creditor?"
>
> "Oh yes, yes," cried the debtor. "You save me from prison and show mercy to me."
>
> "Then," said the benefactor, "you will pay the debt to me and I will set the terms. It will not be easy, but it will be possible. I will provide a way. You need not go to prison." (*Gospel Principles* 65)

Jesus saved them by becoming their creditor! He saved them, but they still must pay him back! This is Mormonism's explanation of the atonement.

This fits with their man-centered plan of salvation and coincides with their teaching of no undeserved blessings and no unilateral covenants. All this weighs heavily on many Mormons. As one former LDS member said, "When I realized that I was saved because of Jesus, it was like someone took a huge boulder off my shoulders."

As stated above, however, what Mormonism means by the atonement is not always readily seen. They often mention it without describing it. It's also getting more difficult because Mormonism is sounding more and more Christian. One striking example is a talk given by Brad Wilcox, a BYU professor. It's entitled "His Grace Is Sufficient." Mormons frequently refer to it to prove they believe in grace just as Christians do.

The key to understanding his talk is seeing his main point: *God's grace is sufficient to get us back into God's presence to be judged.* Wilcox says: "What is left to be determined by our obedience is how comfortable we plan to be in God's presence and what degree of glory we plan on receiving" (35). Note especially the last two phrases: "how comfortable we plan to be in God's presence and what degree of glory we plan on receiving." They reflect the LDS teaching that there are three kingdoms in heaven but only those in the highest (celestial) kingdom will live with God. And living with God in heaven depends on a person's obedience (there's that word again). To sum it up, Wilcox says God's grace is sufficient to get them to the courtroom. But it's up to them to get through the trial.

Jesus as their Example

Mormonism frequently refers to Jesus as their example. "He is the greatest Being to be born on this earth—the perfect example" (*Bible Dictionary* 633). And they point to his example in the context of salvation. "Jesus Christ showed us the way along this covenant path, and we gain eternal life by following His example" ("What Is the Way to Eternal Life?" 43).

In this connection, they often emphasize Jesus' charitable acts more than his death for us. "Peter may have given the best description of the Savior's mortal ministry in five words when he referred to Jesus 'who went about doing good'" (Ballard 10). The passage he quotes, Acts 10:38, is increasingly quoted by LDS leaders.

THE BIBLE'S VIEW

Who Jesus Is

The biblical picture of Jesus is vastly different than the one Mormonism paints. He is God from all eternity. "In the beginning was the Word, and the Word was with God, and the Word was God" (John 1:1). There never was a time when he wasn't God. In the very beginning he was God.

There came a time when he took on a human nature. "The Word became flesh and made his dwelling among us" (John 1:14). But this fact doesn't negate that from all eternity he was God.

The truth that Jesus was God in the beginning also shows the Bible isn't describing a temporal relationship when it calls him the Son of God. In other words, his title as the Son of God doesn't mean the Father existed before him. Rather, it describes an intimate relationship. In addition, this title teaches that the Father and the Son are two distinct persons. (As mentioned in Chapter One, many Mormons misunderstand what Christians believe about the Trinity. They frequently charge us with saying the Father and the Son are the same person.)

As true God, the Son is equal with the Father and demands equal honor. John 5:22-23 is an important passage. "Moreover, the Father judges no one, but has entrusted all judgment to the Son, that all may honor the Son just as they honor the Father. Whoever does not honor the Son does not honor the Father, who sent him." The words "just as" are equivalent to an equal sign. The Son is to be honored exactly as the Father is honored. Whoever does not give him equal honor isn't honoring either him or the Father!

This passage alone condemns Mormonism as a non-Christian religion because it does not give Jesus equal honor with the Father. For example, Mormons don't pray to Jesus. They only pray to the Father through Jesus. "Prayer is a sincere, heartfelt talk with our Heavenly Father. We should pray to God and to no one else" (*Gospel Principles* 35). More than one Mormon has been shocked to hear that Christians pray to Jesus. I remember one LDS woman exclaim to me, "I suppose you also pray to the Holy Spirit!"

Technically, they also don't worship Jesus. I say technically because they frequently say they do. But consider the following statement: "God the Father is the Supreme Being in whom we believe and whom we worship" (*True to the Faith* 74). When this manual describes Jesus, however, there is no mention of worship. In fact, in its article on worship it makes this distinction: "you remember and worship your Heavenly Father and express your gratitude for His

Son, Jesus Christ" (188).

Since they see the Father and the Son as two separate Gods, they can't worship both. If they did, they would be breaking the First Commandment about worshipping only one God.

The Jesus of Mormonism is truly a different Jesus. Having said this, however, we don't think it wise to make their "different Jesus" an emphasis when you talk with Mormons. For most Mormons, these are fighting words. They won't hear anything else you say. In addition, it's much more productive to focus on what the Bible says Jesus did for us. This not only brings to bear the awesome power of the gospel; it also addresses one of the stresses many Mormons experience.

What Jesus Did – Our Substitute

Where Mormonism points to Jesus as their example, the Bible emphasizes he is our substitute. A common way the Bible makes this point is with the little phrase "for us." Here are just a few such passages:

- "God made him who had no sin to be sin *for us*" (2 Corinthians 5:21).
- "He who did not spare his own Son, but gave him up *for us* all—how will he not also, along with him, graciously give us all things?" (Romans 8:32)
- "Christ loved us and gave himself up *for us* as a fragrant offering and sacrifice to God" (Ephesians 5:2)

The little phrase "for us" makes all the difference in the world!

The Bible's message is not "do like Jesus did" but "it's done for us by Jesus."

The Bible uses several different words to describe Jesus' substitutionary death. We have already discussed how Mormonism primarily uses the word atonement. However, the whole KJV New Testament only mentions it once. (Romans 5:11: "We also joy in God through our Lord Jesus Christ, by whom we have now received the atonement.") The Old Testament refers to it much more frequently—often in connection with the Day of Atonement. The New Testament writers prefer words like justify, redeem, reconcile and especially save.

Whatever words the Bible uses, it consistently says Jesus' sacrifice stands alone as the reason God accepts us. We saw this in the last chapter in those passages which state God's grace and man's efforts don't mix. Other verses support this. The following only represent a sampling:

- Romans 3:24: "Being justified freely by his grace through the redemption that is in Christ Jesus" (KJV)
- Titus 3:5: "Not by works of righteousness which we have done, but according to his mercy he saved us" (KJV)
- Hebrews 10:14: "For by one offering he hath perfected for ever them that are sanctified" (KJV)

It's obvious that the Bible bases our salvation solely on Christ's sacrifice for us.

Jesus Lived For Us

But what is all included in his sacrifice? This is something even many Christians are unclear on. Many limit it to his death. But Jesus did more than die for us. He also *lived* for us! With his death, he paid the price for our sins and freed us from the fires of hell. With his life, he perfectly kept all the commandments for us and made us worthy to live in heaven. Since Mormonism lays so much stress on obeying the commandments, the message that Jesus kept the commandments for us is vitally important to share.

Here's a simple way we have learned to teach this. Draw a heart filled with plus signs symbolizing the perfection needed to enter heaven.

Then draw a second heart filled with minus signs. It symbolizes our hearts of sin.

The test is to describe how the heart filled with minus signs becomes the heart filled with plus signs.

Give Mormons this test. Most people, Christians included,

immediately reply that Jesus' death washed our sins away. His death erases the minus signs. But this makes the heart empty. It is still void of plus signs. Ask where the plus signs come from. Most Mormons will point to the good works they do. But that's not what the Bible says. It rules out any role for works in salvation.

The answer is the plus signs represent all the good works Jesus did on our behalf! Galatians 4:4-5 indicates that Jesus came not only to die for us but also to live for us. "But when the set time had fully come, God sent his Son, born of a woman, *born under the law, to redeem those under the law*, that we might receive adoption to sonship" (emphasis added).

Other passages reinforce this, especially those which tell us we have Christ's righteousness or perfection. 1 Corinthians 1:30 simply states that Jesus is our righteousness. Isaiah 61:10 tells us God clothes us with a robe of righteousness. Romans 10:4: "For Christ is the end of the law for righteousness to every one that believeth" (KJV).

We can't encourage you strongly enough to emphasize this with Mormons. Not only have many never heard this, it also addresses one of their principal stresses. Mormonism places so much pressure on them to be obedient! Understanding that Jesus was obedient "for them" offers them incredible relief.

Jesus Reconciled the World to God

"God was reconciling the world to himself in Christ, not counting people's sins against them" (2 Corinthians 5:19). Note carefully what this verse says about the result of Christ's sacrifice. God did not count *the world's* sins against them. This speaks an awesome truth. Unlike Mormonism's message, God did not wait to forgive us until we did something to earn his love.

On the contrary, he took the initiative. He reconciled the world to himself in Christ. So much so that He forgave *the world*.

He could do this because Jesus paid sin's debt in full. Jesus stated this very thing when, on the cross, he declared, "It is finished" (John 19:30). In the original Greek of John's Gospel, it consists of just one word—a word commonly used to mark a bill paid in full. The debt is gone. "And where these have been forgiven, sacrifice for sin is no longer necessary" (Hebrews 10:18).

This doesn't mean all will go to heaven. The Bible is crystal clear that believing Jesus did this is absolutely necessary. "Whoever believes in him is not condemned, but whoever does not believe stands condemned already because they have not believed in the name of God's one and only Son" (John 3:18). But this doesn't mean God waits to forgive us until we believe. Rather, if we don't believe, we don't benefit from the forgiveness.

Even though there is no such thing as a perfect analogy, here's a little story we often tell to make this point. Jason was a very rebellious teen. He consistently flouted his parent's authority. He regularly got into trouble at school. The police had already become familiar with him. One day, however, he did something to his parents that even shocked him. So, he ran away from home. Only his best friend knew where he was. Jason's parents asked his friend to tell him to come home. They had forgiven him! His best friend relayed the message. But regardless of how much he urged Jason to believe it and go home, Jason didn't. So, he remained estranged from his parents.

Do you see the point? Jason's "unbelief" did not alter the fact that his parents had already forgiven him. But his unbelief kept him from enjoying their forgiveness.

So also with us. God has forgiven us. But to benefit from it, we must believe it. (We will take a closer look at faith in the next chapter.)

Highlighting this makes our witness all the more potent. Remember that "if" is a huge word in Mormonism. And it lays a heavy burden on many Mormons. Therefore, when we tell them that God will forgive them *if* they believe, they can easily despair.

It is often much better to tell them: "God has forgiven you! Believe it!" Not only does this take the weight of "if" off their shoulders, it also highlights even more clearly God's amazing love.

> God has forgiven you! Believe it!

CONCLUSION

Are you seeing how drastically different the two bridges across the chasm are? Mormonism's bridge is beyond rickety because it depends so much on human effort. The biblical bridge, however, is rock solid because it is based solely on divine effort.

CHAPTER 5

THE SPIRIT'S WORK

Jesus perfectly built the bridge the Father had planned. It has no flaws. And it needs no additions. He built a complete bridge. And it's indestructible. Nothing can bring it down or even damage it. It is completely sturdy.

The only thing left to do is get people on it. Even here, God didn't leave it up to mankind to get on the bridge themselves. After all, everyone is spiritually dead by nature. Dead people can't do anything. So, the Holy Spirit has to make people spiritually alive. As Jesus told Nicodemus: "Very truly I tell you, no one can enter the kingdom of God unless they are born of water and the Spirit" (John 3:5). Paul put it this way: "No one can say, 'Jesus is Lord,' except by the Holy Spirit" (1 Corinthians 12:3).

Here again, however, Mormonism's emphasis on human effort comes through loud and clear. It's heartbreaking to see how it burdens people every step of the way.

MORMONISM'S VIEW

Companionship of the Holy Ghost

According to D&C 130:22, "the Holy Ghost has not a body of flesh and bones, but is a personage of Spirit." (Because the KJV is their official Bible translation, Mormons still commonly use the title, Holy Ghost.) "He can be in only one place at a time, but His influence can be everywhere at the same time" (*Gospel Principles* 32).

Mormonism distinguishes between the influence of the Holy Ghost and the gift of the Holy Ghost. Anybody can be influenced by him. But only those who are confirmed can receive the gift of the Holy Ghost. (Confirmation is usually closely connected with their baptism into Mormonism. It involves members of the LDS priesthood laying their hands on a person and confirming they are now members of the LDS Church.) Taking it one step further, a major aspect of receiving the gift of the Holy Ghost is having the companionship of the Holy Ghost.

It is not apparent how they reconcile the teaching that countless people can experience this companionship with him being able to be in only one place at a time. This is another example of subjects not worth pursuing since it doesn't bother them.

What they are focused on is remaining worthy to retain his companionship.

> Now that you have the gift of the Holy Ghost, you have the right to the constant companionship of that member of the Godhead *if you keep the commandments*...Even though you have received the

gift of the Holy Ghost, the Spirit will dwell with you
only when you keep the commandments. (*True to the
Faith* 83, emphasis added)

How far do they take this? Pretty far. "The Holy Ghost can be with us only to the degree we keep our lives clean and free from sin" (Pieper 45). "To be worthy to have the help of the Holy Ghost, we must seek earnestly to obey the commandments of God. We must keep our thoughts and actions pure" (*Gospel Principles* 123).

Each statement about keeping the commandments or being free from sin are like another heavy brick added to the load Mormons carry. Making it even worse is that such statements are quite common. Wherever you turn in Mormonism, you quickly run across phrases like "keep the commandments" and qualifications like "if you are worthy." It's no wonder many Mormons throw up their arms in despair and become inactive.

Source of Personal Revelation

A key LDS doctrine says they can receive personal revelations from the Holy Ghost. But only if they are worthy. "All people, if they are worthy enough and close enough to the Lord, can have revelations" (*Teachings of Presidents of the Church: Spencer W. Kimball* 247).

The Holy Ghost gives these revelations through a person's *feelings*. Probably the best-known example is the "burning in the bosom" (D&C 9:8). Some Mormons say they have experienced it as proof that the Book of Mormon is true.

Many LDS members, however, have never felt it. And the LDS

Church is downplaying it. Today they talk more often about listening to the quiet whisperings of the Holy Ghost to guide them in their daily lives. Mormons commonly talk about impressions they received which directed them to do something. A constant refrain of LDS missionaries as they teach their lessons is the question: "How do you feel about that?" It's difficult to overemphasize the vital role feelings play in Mormonism.

This understandably bothers Christians who look to the Bible as the only source of God's revelation. And many want to address this with Mormons. But we discourage that. It doesn't concern most Mormons. In fact, some sincerely feel sorry for us because all we have is the Bible. Pointing out the fickleness of feelings, therefore, usually only frustrates both parties. Here again, we encourage people to stick to those topics which create stress for Mormons; topics like the ones we now turn to.

Repentance and Forgiveness

Repentance and forgiveness are huge topics in Mormonism. Receiving God's forgiveness hinges on a person's repentance. Therefore, it is critical to see how Mormonism defines repentance. The article on repentance in *True to the Faith* is representative. It depicts a six-step "painful process." The fourth step is entitled the "Abandonment of Sin." It quotes D&C 58:43 which says to be repentant, people must forsake their sin. *True to the Faith* then says: "Maintain an unyielding, permanent resolve that you will never repeat the transgression. When you keep this commitment, you will never experience the pain of that sin again" (135).

Abandoning and forsaking are very strong words. A sailor doesn't climb back on a ship he has abandoned. One of the worse things a soldier can do is forsake his post. Mormonism doesn't cut them any slack either. "It is not real repentance until one has abandoned the error of his way and started on a new path. ... The saving power does not extend to him who merely *wants* to change his life" (*Teachings of Presidents of the Church: Spencer W. Kimball* 39).

To make matters even worse, there is this under the sixth step of Mormon repentance, "Righteous Living." "It is not enough to simply try to resist evil or empty your life of sin. You must fill your life with righteousness" (*True to the Faith* 135). *Gospel Principles* elaborates:

> We are not fully repentant if we do not pay tithes or keep the Sabbath day holy or obey the Word of Wisdom. We are not repentant if we do not sustain the authorities of the Church and do not love the Lord and our fellowmen. If we do not pray and are unkind to others, we are surely not repentant. (111)

Abandon and forsake the sin. Empty life of sin and fill it with righteousness. Only then does a person qualify for God's forgiveness. They tell the story of a woman who came to President Kimball because she was despondent over a sin she had committed. He told her: "You *can* be forgiven for this heinous sin, but it will take much sincere repentance to accomplish it" (*Teachings of Presidents of the Church: Spencer W. Kimball* 34).

What constitutes "much sincere repentance"? A few pages later we get the answer. "To every forgiveness there is a condition. The plaster must be as wide as the sore. The fasting, the prayers, the humility *must be equal to or greater than the sin*" (Ibid 38, emphasis added). If the payment must be equal to or greater than the sin, how can they talk about the debt being forgiven? It's not forgiven, it's paid.

In Mormonism, there is no such thing as unconditional forgiveness. "The Lord will not forgive us unless our hearts are fully purged of all hate, bitterness and accusation against our fellowmen" (Ibid 43). "By keeping the commandments and serving others we receive and retain a remission of our sins" (*Preach My Gospel* 63).

These quotes are not obscure or isolated. They could be multiplied many times over. Fewer things are more depressing than reading how Mormonism explains forgiveness.

And fewer things weigh more heavily on Mormons. Sue wrote us in desperation. "I'm Mormon and I need your help. I'm already crying before I type this email." She went on to describe how she had gone to her bishop to confess a sin—something most people would not consider very serious. But she was a very conscientious Mormon and wanted reassurance that she had not done anything to damage her covenant with God. Instead of reassuring her, he quoted the statement above about "the plaster must be as wide as the sore." He then put her on probation for months, not allowing her to receive the sacrament. She was devastated.

> **MORMONISM**
> The fasting, the prayers, the humility must be equal to or greater than the sin.

Her story has a happy ending. She and her family left the LDS Church and joined a Christian Church. In one of her final emails to us, she talked about how their faith was growing by leaps and bounds.

There are many more hurting Mormons like Sue. Many, however, don't reach out for help. Instead, they are slowly being crushed, thinking there is no way God will forgive them. They are more than ready to hear about the biblical message of forgiveness. They don't look for a way to end the conversation which often happens with other topics. Rather they are eager to hear more.

Conversion, Faith, Works

By now, it should come as no surprise that also with conversion Mormonism emphasizes human effort. It describes conversion as a change *in our very nature*. "But it goes beyond behavior, it is a change in our very nature" (*True to the Faith* 41). In this connection, they often quote Mosiah 5:2 from the Book of Mormon. "We have no more disposition to do evil, but to do good continually."

Once again that's a mouthful. Especially when they are told: "You have primary responsibility for your own conversion" (*True to the Faith* 43).

Mormons frequently talk about having faith in Jesus, but what do they have faith in? This is where we need to focus the discussion. The object of their faith is not so much Jesus' saving work for them, but rather his *teachings*. "To have faith in Jesus Christ means to have such trust in Him that we obey whatever He commands" (*Gospel Principles* 103). Are they trusting in what Jesus did for them or are they trusting that following his commands (i.e. moral teachings) is the way to becoming right with God?

Instead of seeing good works as the inevitable result of faith, Mormonism makes them an integral component of faith. "Faith in Jesus Christ is the first principle of the gospel and is more than belief, since true faith always moves its possessor to some kind of physical and mental action" (*Bible Dictionary* 670). Therefore, it rejects that a person can be saved simply by believing in what Jesus did for them. "You cannot receive unconditional salvation simply by declaring your belief in Christ with the understanding that you will inevitably commit sin throughout the rest of your life" (*True to the Faith* 151f).

Summary

Once again, we see how the bridge Mormonism builds to God is built mainly on human effort. Wherever they turn, the finger points at them. "You must be worthy. You must purge your heart of sin. You must change your very nature. You must earn God's forgiveness." God is not just consigned to the background; he is almost taken entirely out of the picture.

This not only puts the spotlight on them, it also puts tremendous pressure on them. Mormonism is a harsh taskmaster and has left many victims in its wake. They desperately need to hear the breathtaking message of all that the Spirit does for them.

THE BIBLE'S VIEW

Conversion

Where Mormonism downplays God, the Bible emphasizes him. We see this as it talks about the amazing work of God, the Holy Spirit. As stated above, even when it came to getting on the bridge, God didn't leave it up to us. Rather, the Holy Spirit put us there.

The Bible teaches this in an outstanding way: by consistently describing conversion as something done not by us, but to us. People are born by the Spirit. As Jesus told Nicodemus: "Very truly I tell you, no one can enter the kingdom of God unless they are born of water and the Spirit. Flesh gives birth to flesh, but the Spirit gives birth to spirit" (John 3:5-6).

Even more striking is the biblical comparison of conversion with resurrection. "But because of his great love for us, God, who is rich in mercy, made us alive with Christ even when we were dead in transgressions—it is by grace you have been saved" (Ephesians 2:4-5). Spiritually dead people can't do anything spiritual including trusting in Jesus' salvation.

That is why the Bible equates conversion not only with resurrection but also with creation. "For God, who said, 'Let light shine out of darkness,' made his light shine in our hearts to give us the light of the knowledge of God's glory displayed in the face of Christ" (2 Corinthians 4:6). "Therefore, if anyone is in Christ, he is a new creation" (2 Corinthians 5:17, ESV).

The tool the Holy Spirit uses to bring people to faith is the gospel, the good news that Jesus lived and died as our substitute. "It is the power of God that brings salvation to everyone who believes" (Romans 1:16). It is not one of several different powerful tools. No, it is THE power God uses. It is the only thing powerful enough to make us alive in Christ. When we urge people, on the basis of the gospel, to believe in Jesus, it is like God commanding the light to shine at creation. Just like his command created the light, so also our appeal to believe creates faith itself! That is how powerful God's Word is!

Therefore, by far the most important thing we can share with Mormons is the gospel. We must be careful that we thoroughly talk about Jesus as our substitute—doing it all for us. Otherwise they will default to thinking of him as their example.

Repentance and Forgiveness

As spelled out above, Mormonism makes forgiveness dependent on repentance. Biblical repentance is a change of mind. It's turning away from trusting in one's own works to trusting in Jesus' work for us. It, too, is a gift of God. 2 Timothy 2:25 is a pertinent passage to remember when witnessing to Mormons. "Opponents must be gently instructed, in the hope that God will grant them repentance leading them to a knowledge of the truth." Note how the hope is that God will *grant* repentance. Even repentance is something God must give.

Forgiveness is a good topic to focus on when sharing the gospel. Even though Mormonism emphasizes a person must work for forgiveness, it hasn't defined it differently. So, there is less chance of talking past each other.

The message of biblical forgiveness is so amazing. When we repent, that is, when we trust in Jesus' perfection rather than our own supposed goodness, we receive God's forgiveness. "In him we have redemption through his blood, the forgiveness of sins, in accordance with the riches of God's grace" (Ephesians 1:7).

God's forgiveness is amazing because it is full and complete. He doesn't leave any debt for us to pay. "You will tread our sins underfoot and hurl all our iniquities into the depths of the sea" (Micah 7:19).

> He does not treat us as our sins deserve
>   or repay us according to our iniquities.
> For as high as the heavens are above the earth,

> so great is his love for those who fear him;
> as far as the east is from the west,
> so far has he removed our transgressions from us.
>
> (Psalm 103:10-12)

Secondly, God's forgiveness is amazing because when he forgives, he also forgets. He doesn't demand that we pay him back. "'Their sins and lawless acts I will remember no more.' And where these have been forgiven, sacrifice for sin is no longer necessary" (Hebrews 10:17-18).

What a striking contrast with LDS forgiveness! Jesus paid the debt of their sin, but they must pay him back. They must go through a painful and long process of repentance before they are forgiven. This process includes forsaking the sin and keeping the commandments!

In startling contrast, the Bible says, "God was reconciling the world to himself in Christ, not counting people's sins against them" (2 Corinthians 5:19). But to receive forgiveness, people must believe it. "Everyone who believes in him receives forgiveness of sins through his name" (Acts 10:43). It's as if I told you I deposited a million dollars in a bank account for you. If you believe me, you go to the bank and become a millionaire. If you don't believe me, you never go. The money is still there, but you gain no benefit from it. Faith is essential. We now turn to it.

Faith and Works

Even when it comes to believing, it's not about what we do. "The person without the Spirit does not accept the things that come from the Spirit of God but considers them foolishness, and cannot understand them because they are discerned only through the Spirit" (1 Corinthians 2:14). The Holy Spirit must create saving faith in us. "No one can say, 'Jesus is Lord,' except by the Holy Spirit" (1 Corinthians 12:3).

It's true that the Bible says faith without works is dead (James 2:26). But it is so important to keep works in their proper place. They are not part of the roots of the tree of salvation. Rather they are the fruit, as the Bible often pictures them (i.e. Galatians 5:22-23). Fruit, not root, is a vitally important distinction.

Ephesians 2:8-10 wonderfully summarizes the relationship of faith and works. "For it is by grace you have been saved, through faith—and this is not from yourselves, it is the gift of God— not by works, so that no one can boast. For we are God's handiwork, created in Christ Jesus to do good works, which God prepared in advance for us to do."

Note how the whole package, including faith, is a gift of God and is not from ourselves. Works have no place in salvation: *"not by works, so that no one can boast."* But then comes verse 10. It first says believers are "created." This refers to the Holy Spirit's work of conversion. Then it says we were created or brought to faith to do good works. In other words, works flow from salvation and faith. Salvation does not flow from works.

CONCLUSION

Let's step back and look again at the different bridges Mormonism and the Bible construct to cross the divide between people and God. They could not be more different! From beginning to end, Mormonism makes humans mainly responsible for building it. God the Father gave them a plan, but he demands that they work that plan. Jesus paid their debt, but they must pay him back. They can experience the companionship of the Holy Ghost, but only if they remain worthy. No matter what part you look at, human effort is paramount in its construction.

The biblical bridge is so different. It's built entirely by God. We contribute absolutely nothing. The Father planned it, motivated not by any worthiness in us, but totally because of his incomprehensible love for us. Jesus paid the entire debt of all mankind and doesn't ask to be repaid. Not only that, he also kept all the commandments perfectly for all people. The Holy Spirit plays the vital role of making people spiritually alive and creating faith in them. From beginning to end, it's all about what God does for people.

Instead of a bridge, Joseph Smith pictured the way to God as a ladder. Climbing it would take a very long time. The climb continues even after death.

> When you climb up a ladder, you must begin at the bottom, and ascend step by step, until you arrive at the top; and so it is with the principles of the gospel—you must begin with the first, and go on until you learn all the principles of exaltation. But it will be a great while after you have passed through the veil [died] before you will have learned them. It is not all to be comprehended in this world; it will be a great work to learn our salvation and exaltation even beyond the grave. (*Teachings of Presidents of the Church: Joseph Smith* [2007] 268)

Instead of a ladder, the biblical bridge is more like an escalator. It does all the work. The Holy Spirit places us on it and carries us home.

PART 3

RETURN TO REACH MORE

PART 3

INTRODUCTION

You recognize the immense chasm between us and God. You see how he bridged that gap. All that remains is how you will use it.

The moment you step on the bridge of Christ alone, God speaks with certainty of the blessings you already have right now. "Whoever hears my word and believes him who sent me *has* eternal life and will not be judged but *has* crossed over from death to life" (John 5:24, emphasis added). Did you notice the tense? You don't have to wait. You already have eternal life as a present possession. It's why the angels rejoice in heaven the moment someone trusts in Christ. While we look forward to one day seeing God face to face in heaven when we finish crossing the bridge, we have his presence within us now. Nothing separates us from his love. Jesus provides "life to the full" (John 10:10).

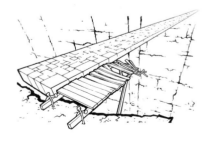

When we as Christians fully appreciate this victory we already have in Christ, it completely transforms our lives. We can approach any trouble with confidence. Even when we face death, we have peace. Scripture describes this transformation as a new creation.

Some Christians are content to travel across the bridge alone until they reach the other side. They forget their purpose in life is to reach even more. Some call out to those still trying to cross the chasm on the failing bridge of Mormonism. Through debate, they may argue that Mormons are on the wrong bridge. This approach might cause some Mormons to realize their bridge is failing. Sadly, it doesn't help them discover the true bridge. Many despair of finding any way to cross the chasm and become agnostic or atheist.

The moment the Spirit placed you on this bridge, you received all the blessings that come with feet securely supported by Christ. There's no need to run to the other side for fear of falling. God promises to walk with you every step of the way. This gives you the confidence to marvel at God's beautiful design and stand in awe of its strength. It also helps you appreciate this bridge will support many more. Those who experience its strength are uniquely equipped to return and reach still more. This is what we'll focus on in part three.

So, you're on the bridge to God. How will you use it?

CHAPTER 6

ANSWERING UNCERTAINTY

Your footing is only as sure as your foundation. When you're relying on an imperfect structure, you will look down and tread lightly with trepidation. You would be hesitant to cross a rope bridge with broken planks. However, you would probably cross a steel overpass on a highway without thinking twice. When you have complete trust in your footing, you look forward with full confidence.

Mormonism places individuals on a precarious bridge. Any sign of trouble shakes this bridge and terrorizes its travelers. It's fastened together by an endless line of impossible demands. Miss even one and the rest come undone. The bridge is unfinished and the final destination is unknown. Uncertainty is the only thing certain in Mormonism.

> Uncertainty is the only thing certain in Mormonism.

God provided an unshakeable bridge. It rests securely on the Father's boundless love. Its travelers are worry free. We know what God has accomplished and the sure hope it brings. With eyes focused on him, we are certain the bridge will bring us home. Speaking with confidence in Christ will expose the uncertainty of Mormonism and help Mormons lift up their eyes to see their Savior.

UNCERTAINTY WHEN TROUBLE STRIKES

Trouble has a way of exposing our focus and the stability of our steps. As an example, many religions claim they know the path to God, but they struggle to answer the problem of suffering. Buddhism teaches suffering is the result of loving too much; love less and you'll suffer less. Other religions teach you must have done something to deserve it; just accept it. Atheism has no answer for suffering; escape it at all costs. These answers fall short.

Mormonism, like other world religions, turns suffering back on Mormons. Since blessings depend on them, they also play a role in the lack of those blessings. This ties God's hands and makes him impersonal. He can't simply bless them out of the goodness of his heart. He is bound by natural law. Mormonism teaches God wants them to be happy and he is cheering them on, but his blessings and love depend on them.

This may allow for a pat on the back when things are going well. However, when the winds of trouble make their bridge sway and creak, it can cause several reactions. The *desperate* throw in the towel. They look down with fear. Because their bridge is collapsing, they get off as quickly as possible. They leave feeling hurt and afraid to approach God. Since they've tried and failed, they believe it is impossible. Many with this reaction are so uncertain about reaching God they stop trying altogether.

Other Mormons have worked so hard on their bridge they don't want to give up now. With the promise that perfection is possible, the *workaholics* just keep trying. They look down to build their next step. Every hardship exposes a weakness in their bridge and drives them to vigorously pick up the pace of laying their rotten planks. They tighten the rusty bolts to reinforce past effort. If they keep busy doing good, they figure it should be enough. After all, what more could they do?

Some just hold on to the bridge they have built. The *weary* can no longer keep working at a frantic pace. They look forward with resignation. They give up on the pursuit of being certain of God's love. Yet, they have invested too much to turn back. Since God is bound by natural law, he will have to reward their past performance. They decide to be content with whatever their past efforts will bring them.

Hardship has a way of exposing the cracks in Mormonism. Understanding whether a Mormon is among the *desperate*, the *workaholics* or the *weary* will impact your approach in reaching them. They all look down from the bridge with fear in their hearts. Trouble often brings this to light.

Yet not every Mormon realizes the gap between them and God. Some are completely unaware. Luke 15, an account you can share with Mormons, demonstrates this contrast in the two sons. The prodigal son eventually realizes his lost condition. His older brother doesn't. They both show they don't understand

> Understanding whether a Mormon is among the *desperate*, the *workaholics* or the *weary* will impact your approach in reaching them.

their father's love.

The younger son squeezes his father for an early inheritance. He cashes out and leaves dear old dad in the dust. When trouble strikes and he bottoms out, he turns back to his father. Yet, looking down, he plans his next steps as a servant. It's only when he looks up into his father's eyes that his concerns are stilled. Now, enveloped in his father's arms, he experiences the depths of this love for the first time. He discovers mercy and forgiveness can only be freely given.

Meanwhile, unseen trouble in the older brother's relationship with his father had been brewing for years and finally boils over. He is incensed with rage. "Look! All these years I've been slaving for you and never disobeyed your orders" (Luke 15:29). On the surface, he appeared as a dutiful son. Everything looked fine. Looking more closely, words like "slaving" and "orders" reveal his relationship was based on fear and obedience. Sadly, the older brother still didn't understand his father's love.

This beautiful chapter was first spoken to older brothers who didn't recognize trouble in their relationship with God. Jesus shows it's possible to rebel through reckless abandon *or* through diligent obedience. When Mormon eyes look down on their actions, they will never look up and see their Savior. So long as they try to earn his love, they can never know it. The chapter ends with an appeal. The dead are alive again. The lost are found. The Father begs older brothers the world around to see what they're missing, fall to their knees beside younger brothers, look up and discover grace.

Tim Keller is credited with saying, "The irony of the gospel is that the only way to be worthy of it is to admit that you're completely unworthy of it." This is where the brilliance of God's love breaks through the darkness. When we finally acknowledge we're lost, we can now be found. When Christ is all we have, we realize Christ is all we need.

This is particularly important to highlight during times of hardship. Suffering exists. Jesus was the most righteous person who ever lived. His record didn't promise him happiness. Instead he experienced poverty, rejection and injustice. God worked through suffering so Jesus could sympathize with us in our weaknesses (Hebrews 4:15).

God also works through suffering today. It moves us to look up and seek refuge in him. There, in the embrace of our Father's loving arms, we discover again his unconditional love. This prompted Paul to boast of his weaknesses because God promised, "My grace is sufficient for you, for my power is made perfect in weakness" (2 Corinthians 12:9).

Trouble reveals our hearts. It exposes the focus of our trust and where we stand with our Father. Trouble strikes fear in those trusting themselves and they run from God. It drives those who know his love to run toward him.

THE UNCERTAINTY OF "IF"

Mormonism keeps eyes looking down by making God's promises conditional. If they fulfill all the requirements, they receive a temple recommend. If they do temple ordinances, they can help themselves and their ancestors progress further. If they continue working in the spirit world after this life, they may be able to reach a higher kingdom of heaven. One condition ties them to another. There is always another string attached.

Some ex-Mormons describe feeling as if they were chasing a

carrot hanging by a stick. If they only want net blessings, then they tithe on their net income, but if they want gross blessings then they must tithe on their gross income. If they are a dutiful son, they will go on a two-year mission. If they are a loving parent, they will do everything possible to keep their family together forever. A higher valued carrot provides greater motivation.

Since God's blessings and his love are inextricably connected, this also makes God's love conditional. For example, Mormonism teaches:

> Come unto Christ, and be perfected in him, and deny yourselves of all ungodliness; and *if* ye shall deny yourselves of all ungodliness, and love God with all your might, mind and strength, *then* is his grace sufficient for you. (*Book of Mormon*, Moroni 10:32, emphasis added)

> While divine love can be called perfect, infinite, enduring, and universal, it cannot correctly be characterized as unconditional. The word does not appear in the scriptures. On the other hand, many verses affirm that the higher levels of love the Father and the Son feel for each of us—and certain divine blessings stemming from that love—are conditional. ("Divine Love" 21f)

Mormons do not understand God's unconditional love. They only know a transactional love. God is relegated to a vending machine. If they make enough payments, they will eventually get what they want. Unfortunately, this vending machine doesn't post the price. They keep inserting more effort and works, but they have no way of knowing if they've almost paid enough or if they're not even close. Conditional love always results in uncertainty.

> **MORMONISM:** TEACHES TRANSACTIONAL LOVE
> **BIBLE:** REVEALS UNCONDITIONAL LOVE

As a smokescreen to distract from this uncertainty, Mormons are encouraged to have a strong testimony. This often includes an emotional experience they perceive to be prompted by the Spirit. This emphasis ultimately leads many to put their faith in faith. Like dew in the sun, this false assurance inevitably evaporates. They are left chasing an endless cycle of trying to prop up their faith. In the end, it creates even more uncertainty.

Sometimes Christians point to the fickleness of feelings. Discounting a Mormon's feelings typically won't win a place in their heart. Instead, we can help them identify the foundation of their feelings.

Faith is only as strong as the object upon which it rests. Much depends on how we see Jesus. If a person only sees Jesus as their example or teacher, they're ultimately putting their faith in their own ability to follow him. This is like building a bridge across the chasm with almost all of its support on our side of the canyon wall! If, however, we see Jesus as our complete substitute, then the object of our faith rests on an outside power apart from ourselves.

Christians experience rock solid assurance because we trust in Christ alone. Jesus said, "It is finished" (John 19:30). That proclamation demolishes any "ifs." The law was fulfilled. Our sins are forgiven. The mission was accomplished. Our Father in heaven didn't send his Son so we might aspire to live with him. He wanted us to know for sure.

AN UNCERTAIN DESTINATION

Mormonism teaches "eternal life is within your reach" (*True to the Faith* 53). The goal is to try their best with the hope the atonement will cover the rest. As mentioned in Chapter 3, one of the most common passages in the Book of Mormon teaches "for we know that it is by grace that we are saved, *after all we can do*" (2 Nephi 25:23, emphasis added). Consider all the question marks this passage creates. A person can always be more gentle, patient, kind, loving, generous, etc. Who can ever say they have accomplished absolutely *all* they could do? This uncertainty impacts their ultimate destination.

Mormons are building a bridge with materials that are flawed with imperfect efforts. Combining their efforts with God's is like trying to weld steel to tin. Even if they were able to fuse them together, their bridge is only as good as the weakest link. Grace *plus* destroys grace. Such a bridge is structurally deficient.

Mormonism tries to alleviate these concerns by making them comfortable with not being ready. It assures they will have more time to build the bridge after this life. This is like someone driving past a "Bridge Out" sign because they were promised everything would work out in the end. Walking across a bridge that is unfinished would be frightening. Trusting their final destination to a God they believe only shows conditional love is terrifying.

If you ask Mormons whether they will live eternally with Heavenly Father, most will share their uncertainty without hesitation. They stake their claim: "I hope so." Some openly acknowledge they are quite sure they won't.

Hope is a word that has been diluted over time. People say, "I hope it doesn't rain" or "I hope my team wins." There are no guarantees. This is nothing more than wishful thinking. When it comes to your eternal destination, you don't want to roll the dice and hope for the best.

The Bible uses the word hope in a completely different way. It is a sure hope. It is an "anchor for the soul" secured behind the curtain (Hebrews 6:19). It is certain because it is based on the bridge Christ built. This bridge is so sturdy and solid, you don't have to wonder whether it will get you across the chasm. You see it reaches across to the other side. This means you don't have to walk with trepidation. You can skip, dance or run across this bridge. In fact, it pleases God when you cross with confidence.

This means the entire life of a Christian can be one of certainty. We're encouraged to "approach God's throne of grace with confidence, so that we may receive mercy and find grace to help us in our time of need" (Hebrews 4:16). God doesn't want to see anything trip us up or rob our confidence along the way. We can go to him with the big things as well as the small. Our prayer life can be vibrant because he listens and answers the prayers of his people.

As a result of this sure and certain hope, we can look forward to Judgment Day. God encourages us to wait with great anticipation. "When these things begin to take place, stand up and lift up your heads, because your redemption is drawing near" (Luke 21:28). It will be a great day of deliverance. Reaching out with this message of hope begins with it deeply planted in us. We can't share something we don't first have ourselves. When God's love fills us with assurance, we are in a better position to witness.

The uncertainty of Mormonism's bridge forces Mormons to tiptoe, look down and carefully watch each step. Our certainty in Christ frees us to step forward in faith with eyes focused on him.

SPEAK WITH CERTAINTY

Undeserved Blessings

When Christians live in the confidence of Christ, others take notice. It's not uncommon for Mormons to take note and even comment: "God really seems to be blessing you. You must be doing something well." This may occur especially when things aren't going well for them.

Even if Mormons don't bring it up, you can. Christians understand blessings are ultimately a gift of God's undeserved love. You can share the amazing things God has done for you in personal ways from a grateful heart. Start by talking about the amazing things God is doing in your life. Be sure to shake off any notion you had anything to do with it—God alone gets the glory.

Even when things aren't going according to your plans, you still have an opportunity to witness. Many of the greatest blessings come from seeking refuge in God during the storms of life. Yet, so often these are hidden from others. Share the powerful testimony of how God worked through a tough time in your life to bless you. You can demonstrate how that hardship has forced you to stop looking down. Describe how God has worked through adversity to draw you even closer in your relationship with him. Speak of how your certainty is not based on present circumstances, but on God's unchanging promises.

A New Approach to God

It's important to help Mormons see there is a new paradigm when it comes to approaching God. The bilateral covenant at Sinai stated: "Now if you obey me fully and keep my covenant, then…you will be my treasured possession" (Exodus 19:5). Despite their efforts, God's Old Testament people were hopelessly unable to accomplish the requirements of the law. Its purpose was to show them their sin.

Mormons are still trying to gain access to God on a bilateral basis. A random selection from the Book of Mormon is likely to yield a host of conditional statements. The emphasis is on keeping their covenant with God. Sadly, this can blind Mormons from clearly seeing God's covenant with us.

Christ fulfilled the bilateral covenant at Sinai. It's critical to help Mormons see Jesus as our substitute. He satisfied the law's demands. He took our punishment for us. He lived perfectly in our place. We now have access to God through the new, unilateral covenant. The biblical emphasis is on what Christ has done.

When Mormons inevitably try to add a condition, remind them Christ already fulfilled the law for them. Jesus removed the "if." This allows them to read the promises of God in a whole new light. It effectively cuts the string on the carrot they are chasing so they can see the blessings found in Christ right now.

A Glimpse into God's Heart

Some Mormons may respond with confusion. Why would God give blessings freely? It doesn't make sense. After all, what's in it for him? These questions are common because Mormons don't understand the amazing love we know as grace.

We all want to be loved. A parent is much more pleased with the child who cleans their room out of gratitude rather than obligation. There would be no satisfaction in asking a robot to the dance; true love can't be programmed. The deeper love we crave isn't experienced under compulsion. It is only possible when love is a choice.

"God so loved the world" (John 3:16). This is a love of choice. We didn't deserve it. We could never repay it. It has nothing to do with who we are. It has everything to do with who God is. The Bible doesn't say God *has* love. It says God *is* love (1 John 4:16). Love is his nature, his message and his mission. He created us to be objects of his love. He's not focused on what we have to offer. What he really wants is *us*.

> God isn't focused on what we have to offer. What he really wants is us.

Grace is an unavoidable stumbling block for Mormons. Mormonism pictures it as the easy way out. Many ex-Mormons would disagree. It was much easier trusting in their own effort than to step forward in faith and trust in Christ alone. Of course, after tasting grace, they realize what they were missing all along.

We pray Mormons would one day "grasp how wide and long and high and deep is the love of Christ" (Ephesians 3:18). The Spirit alone has the power to open their eyes and change their hearts. Therefore, share that message trusting in the power of the Word through which the Spirit works.

Speak Mormonese

As we speak the Word, it is important to do so clearly. Many Christians can talk to Mormons and, at first, they seem to agree. Later, however, they recognize the significant differences and can become frustrated. This is because Mormonism uses a Christian glossary with very different definitions. This language, unique to Mormonism, is sometimes described as Mormonese.

Bridging the gap between Mormonese and what we might call Christianese requires translation. When Mormons speak of grace, they picture God's enabling power to help those who help themselves. Instead speak of God's "no strings attached" love because of who he is. Mormonism teaches the atonement makes forgiveness *possible*. Focus on how atonement makes forgiveness *complete* (Hebrews 10:18). Mormonism describes repentance as "a painful process" (*True to the Faith* 133). You can describe the transformational joy that follows when turning from trust in self to trust in Christ alone. Instead of heaven, speak of living eternally with Heavenly Father. To understand how to navigate more of the different definitions, check out the Dictionary of Mormonese on tilm.org.

Speaking their language also means sharing the Word heart to heart. Emotions play an important role in how Mormons perceive spiritual truths. Many well-intentioned Christians start with matters of the mind and become discouraged when these contradictions don't trouble Mormons.

For this reason, we encourage you to proclaim before you explain.

Take God's promises and describe the impact it has had on you. Overflow with the joy you have trusting in Jesus as your substitute. Describe the peace of living in complete forgiveness. Speak of the confidence of knowing you have life with God now and forever. When you speak with emotion, you're talking to Mormons on their wavelength.

As you speak personally, it's unlikely someone will argue about your feelings. Instead of a *this* against *that* posture, you're attracting them to lean in and learn more. Many Mormons are genuinely curious about why we feel that way, which then opens the door to share the reason for our hope. Proclaiming heart to heart often opens the door to explaining mind to mind. Then, you can point to the unchanging biblical truths upon which your emotions rest.

Know Where You're Going

Part of speaking clearly means keeping the main thing the main thing. If we major on minor points, it can lead us down rabbit holes. We don't want to argue with Mormons about the rivets they're using to build their bridge. We want them to cross on the bridge Christ built. For this reason, we want to keep the focus on the big picture matters of salvation.

It can be helpful to start at the end and work backwards. Ask Mormons to picture themselves standing before God on Judgment Day. What will it be like to stand on their own record? How will they feel seeing the film reel of their entire life played back? Is the quality and quantity of their work really enough? This perspective exposes uncertainties and shows Mormonism's bridge can't go the distance.

Then speak of your confidence. It is the day of deliverance when

God's people lift their eyes to the skies. We look forward with great anticipation: "I just can't wait until Judgment Day." On that great day, we will stand on Christ's perfect record. We have an airtight case and we already know the verdict.

Susan left Mormonism, divorced her husband and spent the next thirteen years very angry. To fill the void, she turned to New Age and other occult religions, but she couldn't seem to find the truth she was seeking. When her mother was on her deathbed, Susan was touched by the comfort and assurance she displayed. By resting entirely on God's promises, her mother was 100% certain she was going to see Jesus in heaven because she was freely and fully forgiven. This had quite an impact on Susan.

She longed for the faith of her mother. Over the course of three years, she vigorously studied the Bible with the help of her brother. She worked through the false teaching of Mormonism that had been deeply ingrained in her. During this long journey, the Spirit gave her faith in her Savior. With any journey involving the heart, the length of time is overshadowed by the joy experienced in finally coming home and resting in the arms of Jesus.

Christ alone can provide the certainty Mormons seek. God can use you to help them look up and discover his love.

CHAPTER 7

DROPPING THE BAGGAGE

When you have a trip coming up, you plan what to pack. If you're attending a wedding, you'll bring along different attire than if you're simply a tourist. Variable weather calls for additional layers. The longer the trip, the more bags you bring. You want to be ready for every situation.

Mormons work hard to be as prepared as possible for their life's journey. On the surface, they can give the impression they have everything under control. A closer look reveals they are often burdened by all the baggage they carry.

This life's journey has an all-inclusive destination. "The LORD Almighty will prepare a feast of rich food for all peoples, a banquet of aged wine" (Isaiah 25:6). God provides everything we need. With the robe of Jesus' righteousness, he even gives us clothes to wear. When we understand God has made all the preparations, it changes everything. We're free to travel light through life. In fact, we don't have to carry any bags along the way. When Mormons discover Jesus already made their preparations, they too will be able to leave their baggage behind.

WHO IS AT THE CENTER?

Mormonism is human-centered. In the end, it's all about the individual. Mormons will do many things for God, but their purpose is to earn his favor. Just as an engine is at the center and ultimately powers each component in a car, Mormonism makes the individual the center of gravity and depends on them to power their salvation. This makes it easy for Mormons to become trapped under the weight of "me."

Christianity is centered on God. The focus is on what God has already done for us. This takes the pressure off us. Jesus is enough. He powers our salvation. Knowing that truth is liberating. What follows are a few ways to keep God as the focus. This can help Mormons drop their baggage of fear and approach God with freedom.

Identity Crisis

Mormons are desperate to be worthy. The concept of worth, by definition, is determined by another. For example, you may have an idea of how much your home is worth. An appraiser can help by providing an assessment. Yet, its ultimate value is based on what a potential buyer is willing to pay. Worthiness for Mormons is determined by leaders in the LDS church.

Pause to consider what's happening here. This is not merely ascribing cost to some inanimate object like a home. *Mormonism determines the value of a person.* It doesn't use a monetary scale, but a spiritual scale of even greater significance. For those of us on

> Mormonism determines the value of a person.

CHAPTER 7: DROPPING THE BAGGAGE

the outside, this undoubtedly raises red flags of warning. For those trapped in Mormonism, however, it creates a heavy weight. Many Mormons dread these meetings with their leaders. Some resent that another person asserts the power to determine their worth.

This model that some are worth more than others is then applied to how God values people. This should not be surprising. It is a common approach in our world today. Most don't even realize they adopt it, but it is revealed in phrases like "that person deserves to go to hell" or their loved one was "hopefully good enough for heaven." This mindset flows naturally from the human heart. The difference with Mormons is they don't simply assume they will be fine. They must *prove* their worth. They are desperate to receive value from God.

In Mormonism, the spotlight is always on the individual. Mormons are constantly looking at themselves to evaluate their worth. Tragically, this human-centered approach takes the focus off of God. Now they become the center of gravity in their spiritual world. They carry the heavy burden of building up a substantial spiritual resume.

This emphasis makes it difficult for Mormons to understand or even be attracted to the gospel. Everything has centered on them. They've made spiritual investments they thought would help them every step of the way. They've put in so much work. They've been clinging to their efforts for so long, it's challenging to conceive of any other way. Don't be surprised when they receive the gospel message you share with disgust rather than delight.

Yet, through the gospel the Spirit has the power to melt their frozen grip. He loosens their hands by helping Mormons see what they're clinging to still isn't enough. You can help them discover what it looks like to cling instead to Christ. One ex-Mormon put it this way, "It is harder than you'd think to give up on works, but once you hand it over to God you finally experience relief."

This only happens when we are found in Christ. It doesn't simply occur by following Christ or taking on his name. It goes far deeper. It's who we now are. We leave our previous identity behind. We are no longer that person. Instead, we are so entirely covered with Christ that his record is now ours. This is why Scripture describes believers in exalted terms like "righteous" and "saints." He is now our identity. "Therefore, if anyone is in Christ, the new creation has come: The old has gone, the new is here!" (2 Corinthians 5:17).

These promises completely change a person's relationship with God. Picture those on the failing bridge of Mormonism now dropping their baggage of self-worth. They no longer need to strive to earn love; they now know they are a precious child of God. They don't have to wonder where they stand; they are in his family. Jesus' open arms on the cross proved our value. In Christ, we know who we are and, more importantly, whose we are.

Why Am I Here?

Some cultures place a tremendous emphasis on academics. Students memorize facts and study to pass a final test. The results determine their rank within the class and have significant implications for their future career.

Mormonism teaches their time here on earth is a test.

> Our mortal life is designed by a loving God to be a test and source of growth for each of us. You remember God's words regarding his children at the creation of

the world: "And we will prove them herewith, to see if they will do all things whatsoever the Lord their God shall command them" [Abraham 3:25]. ("Try, Try, Try" 90)

The commandments are the test God has provided. Their earthly life is particularly important because it is their opportunity to overcome the temptations of the flesh unique to having a mortal body.

When your sole purpose is on passing a test, you're likely to highlight areas where you're doing well. Picture the student who shows his report card to his parents. He points out the good grades, while his thumb covers up the bad ones. In Mormonism, focusing on sin is often just a distraction. The sin that matters most is not progressing on the plan of salvation. "We come to earth for the purpose of growing and progressing. This is a lifelong process" (*Gospel Principles* 107). One Mormon put it this way: "It doesn't matter where you start as long as you keep improving."

> **MORMONISM**
> The sin that matters most is not progressing on the plan of salvation.

Many Mormons believe they are actually doing pretty well. We've heard more than one Mormon say, "I keep all the commandments." If you examine this in the light of Scripture, some may become agitated. They don't want you to disrupt the artificial harmony because their entire house of cards may come crashing down.

A skeptical Mormon might ask you, "What, then, is our purpose?" For some, it is a defensive mechanism to protect their foundation. If they hear "works don't matter" they will cite passages to support their point and then the conversation typically ends.

We rightly teach works are *not necessary for salvation*. We want to be careful, however, not to say works are *not necessary*. "For it is by grace you have been saved, through faith—and this is not from yourselves, it is the gift of God—not by works, so that no one can boast. For we are God's handiwork, created in Christ Jesus to do good works, which God prepared in advance for us to do" (Ephesians 2:8-10). Grace sets us free. Now we can show true love for God and others. Now we want to follow his commandments. We do this not out of obligation, but out of thanks.

Some searching Mormons struggle with the concept that Jesus has done it all. In an effort to leave Mormonism behind, many abandon all of the rules they were taught. Giving up one ethical system before finding another leaves them floundering. Some throw all caution to the wind. They discover newfound freedom, but they don't yet have the spiritual maturity to handle it. It is vitally important to speak clearly so they look only to Christ.

You can help transitioning Mormons navigate these difficult waters. Previously they did good works to please God. When God is already pleased with them through faith in Jesus, they will naturally ask, "What now?" They are experiencing a completely different paradigm. Be prepared to walk patiently with them. It will take time for them to adapt. Now they are not only struggling with identity, but also with their purpose. Help them drop the baggage of performance. Lift their eyes to God's vision for their lives.

Dropping their baggage doesn't mean they will do nothing. Instead, it transforms their activity. Previously, they attended events, served others and gave gifts to seek God's blessing. Now in Christ they may do similar activities, but it overflows from the blessing God has already given them. This change allows Mormons to be a part of something bigger than themselves. When they understand God's plans, they will have a greater appreciation for God at the center and find new, deeper meaning in life.

Under Pressure

Imagine a pressure cooker without a release valve. The steam would build up yet have no way to escape. It would quickly become dangerous and eventually lead to an explosion.

This is where many Mormons find themselves. The weight of being worthy combined with the strain of trying to pass the test creates tremendous pressure. Now add the weight of being in a state of constant scrutiny. It's like having a camera monitor your every activity. It's unnerving even to consider. Every angle of their life is scrutinized. From family, other members, leaders or even God, all eyes are on them. There is no escape.

For this reason, many have described their time in Mormonism as wearing a mask. They desperately try to be someone else. The emphasis to highlight the good in their life forces them to keep up appearances. This stems, in part, from a common phrase in Mormonism: "the best are blessed." The better their life appears, the better they must actually be. Many Mormons feel the pressure to pursue professional careers to project a mask of success. If they can build their own empire and their family is well-dressed, it would be further indication of just how good they are.

The collective pressure of Mormon culture leads many to hide their struggles. They have a very high rate of suicide and drug abuse.

There really isn't an outlet to be authentic about their challenges. Some may be reluctant to open up even to their own family.

Many Mormons are isolated and hurting under this pressure. See them as victims of Mormonism. You can be the outlet where they feel comfortable and open up. In fact, Mormons are much more likely to share their struggles with Christians than with other Mormons. You can share how a God-centered life takes the pressure away.

When Christ is at the center, everything changes. It no longer revolves around who we are or what we have done. Now it's all about who God is and what he has done.

Among other things, this changes the concept of worth. Before it was about them pursuing God's favor. Now, centered on Christ, the focus of their entire lives is ascribing worth to God, i.e. worship. "In view of God's mercy, offer your bodies as a living sacrifice, holy and pleasing to God—this is your true and proper worship" (Romans 12:1). How they live now shows how great God is.

This new worldview also changes their perspective on glory. They have no need to please others and they have nothing to prove. It's not about building their kingdom, but his. When their focus is on proclaiming the wonderful works of God, he alone gets the credit.

When the Spirit helps Mormons see their new identity and purpose in Christ, they finally recognize God as their center of gravity. Now they can drop the baggage of trying to prove themselves worthy and step forward in faith.

A COMPASSIONATE APPROACH

Listen and Love

Many Christians think witnessing begins with speaking. Since they are not sure what to say, they quickly give up. God gave us two ears and one mouth for a reason. He intends for us to listen and soak up his Word so we're overflowing with a message to share. He also intends for us to listen to those we seek to reach so we know how best to share it.

For example, a Mormon who is confident in his own self-righteousness will need to hear a message of the law, so he realizes the futility of his "filthy rags" (Isaiah 64:6) efforts. A Mormon who already realizes she can never be good enough needs the healing of the gospel to see herself covered in Christ. A conversation with a true believing Mormon should stay focused on a simple message of sin and salvation. A conversation with a doubting Mormon may cover a variety of topics to answer their questions. Since Mormons cover such a wide spectrum, it's important to first listen.

Listening also builds trust. People don't care how much you know until they know how much you care. Be vulnerable with Mormons. Be open about your struggles. Don't be sensational but be real. Point to how lost you would be without Christ. This authenticity provides a safe place for them to open up.

Active listening involves asking questions. You can start by getting to know them personally as the unique individual God has made them. Ask about their interests or different callings within the church. Show respect for their sensibilities and their values. Treat each Mormon as a person, not a project. Love them. Look for ways to spend time with them.

When you listen to and love Mormons, you will learn where they are finding their identity and purpose. You will also discover their struggles. A surgeon takes time to discuss symptoms and makes a careful diagnosis in order for the scalpel to bring healing with precision. A Christian witness does the same.

Transform Stress Points to Rest Points

Many Christians focus on what bothers them about Mormonism. For this reason, they begin focusing on topics like the nature of God, additional Scriptures or Joseph Smith. These topics don't bother Mormons. Mormonism spends a great deal of time immunizing them against the most commonly discussed Christian issues.

Another common mistake is setting Mormonism against Christianity or Mormons against Christians. This approach leads to a scenario where matters are resolved by the best debater. It often results in people throwing their hands in the air and each side leaving frustrated. There is another way. Instead, set Mormons against Mormonism. Repeat the stress points they've shared. Let the scalpel of the Word cut to the heart and expose how their pain stems from the "impossible gospel" of Mormonism.

> Set Mormons against Mormonism.

Paul was "greatly distressed" (Acts 17:16) to see all the idols in Athens. Yet, he didn't make *his* distress the focus. Instead, he found something which bothered them. He focused on their stress point. Even with all their statues of gods, deep down they were still concerned about the potential of missing one. So, Paul addressed the unknown God.

Perfectionism

Perfectionism distresses many Mormons. One of the most commonly used Bible passages in Mormonism is "Be perfect, therefore, as your heavenly Father is perfect" (Matthew 5:48). We frequently hear Mormon moms tell us, "You don't know how hard it is to raise perfect kids." These expectations can be crippling. It can feel like a never-ending rat race.

Emphasize your status in Christ. "By one sacrifice he has made perfect forever those who are being made holy" (Hebrews 10:14). You are covered in his perfection. This is not something you need to attain. It's already accomplished. When you tell a Mormon you are already perfect right now, they will scratch their heads with wonder to learn more about how this can be. Point them back to the text where they will discover this status is only possible when we're covered with Christ alone.

Forgiveness Someday

Mormonism teaches forgiveness depends on an individual. "You cannot be saved *in your sins*" (*True to the Faith* 151). It does not teach God forgives and forgets. In fact, it teaches that committing a sin again will cause God to remember the first occurrence and punish them for not being truly sorry. Forgiveness is conditional on their repentance, which includes abandoning the sin. For these reasons, most Mormons hope to have forgiveness someday (usually after this life).

Speak about the peace of forgiveness you *have* right now. "In him we have redemption through his blood, the forgiveness of sins"

(Ephesians 1:7, emphasis added). Forgiveness is a present reality because it was won by Christ. Where God forgives, he also forgets (Jeremiah 31:34). Any attempt to make a payment now is not only unnecessary; it is impossible. "Where these have been forgiven, there is no longer any sacrifice for sin" (Hebrews 10:18). In fact, trying to earn forgiveness is a great offense to God because it says Jesus' payment is not enough. Patiently help Mormons to see forgiveness is found in Christ alone.

Living eternally with Heavenly Father

Many Mormons will tell you they believe in salvation by Jesus' atonement. They use Mormonism's definition of salvation as resurrection. "We will all be resurrected. We will all go back to God's presence to be judged. What is left to be determined by our obedience is how comfortable we plan to be in God's presence and what degree of glory we plan on receiving" (Wilcox 35). In Mormonism, what happens at the judgment depends entirely on them. Unless they measure up to qualify for the highest kingdom of glory, the only time they will be in God's presence is for the judgment. How frightening!

Speak with confidence about how the Bible says your story ends. Jesus' resurrection doesn't just get us to the courtroom. It gets us through it. He "was raised to life for our justification" (Romans 4:25). The payment was accepted. In fact, the Bible doesn't describe living with God as something we will have someday. It is a present possession. "The one who believes *has* eternal life" (John 6:47, emphasis added). What Mormonism holds out as the ultimate prize, i.e. living eternally with Heavenly Father, we already have when we stand on Christ alone.

Amanda was baptized at age 8 into Mormonism. This is when she first felt weighed down. She would later participate in baptisms for the dead where she was told people would come back from the spirit world to thank her. Nothing happened. She felt she must be doing something wrong yet couldn't share it with others. This created even more significant burdens.

Amanda wore a mask in Mormonism. She knew she was supposed to have a relationship with God, but never felt he was there. During these years she didn't feel like she really had an identity. Her life revolved around the activity of helping others. She felt like a shell of a person. Her ultimate goal was to get her body to heaven.

Amanda left Mormonism when she was 17. She found her new identity in Christ. He filled in everything that was previously vacant. In Christianity, her focus now was much more on her soul and the unique person God made her to be. Now she had a relationship with God and knew she was going to heaven.

Many of Amanda's family members are still trapped in Mormonism. She has, at times, entered an LDS church for family events. Each time she felt the pull of impossible expectations. She describes an evil presence pressing down on her shoulders. She has to be careful not to become burdened again by additional baggage. She now describes her new life as a Christian as dropping everything with a breath of relief.

Many of the stress points Mormons experience revolve around their efforts. This is because Mormonism is human-centered. They carry around endless baggage. Unfortunately, there is always more to do, so the promises of Mormonism are evasive. No Jesus, no peace. When everything centers instead on the preparations Jesus has already made for us, God's promises are guaranteed. Know Jesus, know peace. By setting their eyes on Christ alone, the Spirit can use you to help Mormons drop their bags one by one and step forward burden-free.

CHAPTER 8

WALKING TOGETHER

By now you understand just how vastly different Mormonism is from Christianity. Your heart breaks for souls who have been caught in this web of deception. You share your concern for those who ask God to judge them on their own record. You proclaim the transformational change to your identity and the purpose that comes from standing on the gospel promises in Christ. Over time your Mormon family and friends may open up about their struggles. It is important to put yourself in their shoes, so you are prepared to walk with them on the journey out of Mormonism.

Imagine beginning to realize the bridge you're on is failing. You would be terrified! The shock leads you to freeze in a state of confusion. This is what countless Mormons experience. They don't know where to turn!

As mentioned in chapter six, the *desperate* try to get off as quickly as possible. Who can blame them? They don't want to be on the bridge when it comes crashing down. They run back to the beginning of the chasm. For years they were told they belonged to the one true church. Now they look back at the bridge of Mormonism with contempt. Tragically, they don't look for another bridge and they give up hope of ever getting across. Two of three who leave Mormonism stay here and never discover the bridge to God (Cooperman).

The *family-focused* may realize the weakness of Mormonism's bridge, but they're afraid of leaving loved ones behind. Stepping away would create a barrier between them and immediate family members. Extended family could perceive them as a threat to their faith and keep their distance. They risk losing their entire community. The pressure to stay is enormous. It's comfortable. These Mormons may sweep their fears under the rug and ignore their struggles in order to keep family peace.

The *searching* are determined to make it across to God. They want to plant their next steps on a solid bridge that will carry them home. They typically struggle with trusting spiritual leaders initially because they've been led astray before. Their first steps on a new bridge can be filled with trepidation. They may continue to search the landscape for other bridges. They even struggle to trust themselves because they recognize their own feet once led them down the wrong path.

Mormons in each of these camps can feel isolated and all alone. The *desperate* often find themselves in a "fend for yourselves" crowd and lack deep connection. The *family-focused* have demonstrated their need for close relationships, but still yearn for a relationship with God. The *searching* are filled with questions and need someone to guide them. Each presents a unique opportunity for Christians to reach out their hand and walk with them.

A GUIDE FOR THE JOURNEY

Be Present

The Great Commission starts with "go." We're not told to wait for them to come to us. He tells us to leave the ninety-nine in order to go and find the one. The lost need someone to show them the way. God continues to do that through people like you. Going to a Mormon starts by being present.

We don't want to be overbearing, but it is important Mormons know they can turn to us. Verbalize your commitment to walk with them. Follow up with check-ins to show your intention goes beyond kind words. Ask how they're feeling. There is so much for them to process. Let them know they don't have to face this alone.

> Let them know they don't have to face this alone.

The journey out of Mormonism is a grieving process. They will mourn the loss they are experiencing. Relationships may be stressed or fractured. If their spouse does not also leave Mormonism, they may feel a strain on their marriage and it may even end in divorce. Their children may remain in Mormonism. The loss is deeply personal because they are separated from their roots and place in life. They even struggle to understand their reflection looking back in the mirror. Help them identify their emotions. Validate their loss. Anyone on this journey will experience pain. Being present involves a listening ear and sometimes a shoulder upon which to cry.

Transitioning Mormons also need words of encouragement. Help them discover their new identity in Christ. Begin by recognizing on our own we are not as good as we once imagined. Now, through

Christ, we're much more than we could have dreamed possible. Point to the terms the Bible uses to describe those covered in Christ like "righteous," "saints" and "forgiven." Speak life into them.

It is common for Mormons to experience anger along the journey. They regret the resources lost in tithing and volunteering. Some become experts in the historical inaccuracies of Mormonism, which further fuels the fire of rage. It's easy to become bitter and fall into a downward spiral. Many get stuck in anger and don't realize Mormonism is still holding power over them. Ask penetrating questions to help them see this is not the place they want to stay. Walk them through how to let go and hand over their hurt to God.

Most will face fear. In some communities, they could lose their job. Many are afraid of the future and the unknown. They may be afraid of being deceived again, so they're reluctant to join any church. This is similar to getting food poisoning at one restaurant and then never eating at any other restaurant again. Provide perspective. Talk through each fear. Answer each with the promises of God. Only in him will they discover they have no need to fear.

Be authentic. Invest time to get to know them personally. Look for activities to do together that go beyond studying the Bible. Be intentional about building up your relationship. Ask to pray for them and then do it immediately in their presence. Doing so not only shows how much you care, but, more importantly, shows how much God cares. The prayer of a Christian demonstrates the close personal relationship we have with God. It illustrates in action the direct access we have to God.

Mormons can benefit from a guide to help them navigate an array of difficult emotions. Be present so they know they are not alone. Sometimes you'll simply serve as a sounding board and a friend. Keep pointing them to our greatest friend in Jesus. He alone can provide healing for the hurt.

Be Patient

God tells us to go. There is an urgency to reach the lost. There is also a need to then "stay" with persistence. Witnessing is not a one and done proposition. "[The Lord] is patient with you, not wanting anyone to perish, but everyone to come to repentance" (2 Peter 3:9). Consider the patience God has shown you. He intends to show that same patience in action through us as we walk together with Mormons.

We know that walking with a Mormon can be difficult. Because you've taken the time to be present with them, you've grown to care about them personally. It can be painful to see them struggle along the journey. Yet, patience is essential because everyone travels this road at a different pace. Some seeds grow quickly. Others will take time. The process cannot be forced nor would you want it to be. Provide a gentle, recurring nudge in love. Pushing too hard could push them away. Remember this is ultimately between them and God. We're just a guide on the side.

Most Mormons will also experience a truth crisis. They have been told many plain and precious truths have been lost from the Bible. You can share that archaeological and textual discoveries demonstrate the accuracy of the Hebrew Old Testament. The abundance of copies and close dating to Christ attest to the reliability of the Greek New Testament. Yet, someone can't be argued into faith. Help them see the tremendous respect Jesus showed the Scriptures. Urge them to view the Scriptures in the same light. They've heard the authoritarian leader say, "Believe it because I said so!" Now they need an encourager who will patiently point to God's promises and wait on the Spirit for those promises to take root.

Mormons have not been taught how to study the Bible. Provide them with a modern translation with cross-references. Begin by studying together. You might start in the gospels and focus on simply reading the Word at face value. Encourage them to ask questions. Provide background and show them the importance context has on the meaning of a verse. Allow those verses which are easier to understand to shed light on more difficult ones. Point out the tenses of verbs so they see what God has already done and the blessings we now have. Over time, they will rely on the Bible for their foundation instead of feelings. These words of life have the power to set them free from the toxic lies of Mormonism. It can take years to unravel Mormonism. Be patient.

Some transitioning Mormons will also struggle to understand the nature of God. Previously, Mormonism's view of god made sense from a logical perspective. Now, they struggle to grasp the Trinity. You can emphasize how three persons in one God demonstrates the relational nature of God and his love in action from eternity. Help them see how a sovereign, infinite God would be so much grander than us; it makes sense he would be incomprehensible. It's comforting to know we have a big God who can do big things. That truth helps us stand back in awe together at the distance God traveled to build the bridge to us. Direct them in the text to see the mystery of the Trinity is the only biblical view of God.

It will be critical for Mormons to connect to a biblical Christian community. Starting with a small group Bible study can allow for deeper relationships, see how others personally apply Scripture and provide a safe place to ask questions. Mormons have been taught the church is an institution and will struggle to navigate different denominations. Share various reasons for differences among Christians. No visible church is perfect. Emphasize the importance of finding a church that is true to the Bible and focused on our mission. Instead of seeing the church as an institution, help them see the one true church is the body of Christ, i.e. all people who trust in him alone. Here they can begin to celebrate the family of God and find support from others.

Encourage them to get involved in a Christian community so their commitment will grow. Previously, they received callings for which they may not have had gifts. Now they can explore their passion and tap into their unique gifts to glorify God and serve others. Many will want to reach their Mormon family and friends. Activate them in sharing truths they have learned and the comfort they've discovered. They don't need to have all the answers. Philip's invitation was simple: "Come and see" (John 1:46).

It takes time for a person to process a changing worldview. Be prepared that there will be a pull to return to the failing bridge of Mormonism. Don't be surprised if they appear to back track along the way. They want to please family members who may be actively trying to reach them. They may miss the relationships of their Mormon friends. Even after they leave Mormonism, they may still identify culturally as a Mormon. Don't give up hope. Continue to patiently walk with them. Reflect the unconditional love they can only find in Christ.

SPEAK CONFIDENTLY

Stay Focused

Many Christians are reluctant to witness to Mormons. We think we first need to become an expert in Mormonism. While it can be helpful to know where Mormons are coming from, it can also be easy to drown in the details. Too much emphasis on Mormonism can lead to unproductive rabbit holes and take our focus further away from the central message we want to share.

Focus on the Father's love. Mormons struggle to fathom the love of their heavenly Father. They're trying hard to gain his favor. Show how this approach actually limits his love. The Bible challenges us to picture an abundant love that overflows. It changes us. "See what great love the Father has lavished on us, that we should be called children of God! And that is what we are!" (1 John 3:1). Speak of the confidence you have trusting in the Father's loving plan.

Help them see Jesus. Mormonism minimizes Jesus' person and work. Point to his saving work as our substitute. Emphasize he lived and died for us and we are now credited with his record. Direct them to see his work is complete and the rock-solid confidence this brings. When they understand what Jesus has done for them, they will be better positioned to see who Jesus is and trust him alone.

Encourage them to find assurance from the Spirit. Mormons are taught continued companionship of the Spirit depends on them. This perspective results in a distant god. Highlight how God is so close he now dwells within us. His relentless pursuit placed our feet on the bridge to God. He also provides continued strength and guides us along the way. This allows us to rest securely knowing God is with us.

The Father sketched out the plan. Jesus built a flawless bridge. The Spirit now guides our steps. You know these truths personally. You have a message to share. Witnessing to Mormons is accessible to anyone when you stay focused on the great works of God.

Find Joy in Your Role

Would you rather fight Satan's grip on Mormons with a butter knife or with a sword? The answer is obvious, right? Yet, many Christians opt for the butter knife of human reason and logic.

Why? Sometimes this happens when we see Mormons as the enemy. When we start off on a defensive foot, it's very difficult to adjust later. This approach leads many to debate Mormonism where the ultimate focus is on winning an argument over winning a soul. These Christians may be well-intentioned, but the focus is on telling Mormons they're on the wrong bridge. We may even convince them, but when we haven't also helped them see the bridge Christ built for us, we've just paved the path to hopelessness.

This approach can also rob the Christian of joy. When you're so focused on saying things just the right way, you will be nervous during your discussions. You'll wrap up with regret and second guess yourself with ways you should have done better. This inadvertently places the focus on you.

Even if someone was argued out of Mormonism into Christianity, it's unlikely to stick. Subjecting everything to human intellect will pose problems when you encounter matters that can only be known by faith. Someone who is argued into a position can be argued out of it

Trust in the sword of the Spirit!

when a more convincing rational argument comes along.

We believe there is a better way.

Trust in the sword of the Spirit! It has the power to cut through barriers and change hearts. "For I am not ashamed of the gospel, because it is the power of God that brings salvation to everyone who believes" (Romans 1:16). The original Greek word for power is where we get our English dynamite. I've heard some say, "That Mormon has a heart set in stone and would never change." Light off the dynamite of the gospel next to their heart and you'll have a spectacular show! Make sure your witness relies on that power.

Take note of the process. "Everyone who believes" comes to faith through the gospel. There is no other way. God doesn't strike people with lightning. Instead he wrote an amazing love story and made us the object of his love. So, know your tool and reach for it first each time.

It's also important to know your role. He called us to be his witnesses, not lawyers. A witness simply speaks of what they saw, experienced, know. In a court of law, they're instructed not to go beyond that. In fact, if you use persuasive language as a witness, someone will object.

We plant and water the seeds. God alone makes faith grow (1 Corinthians 3:6). Understanding this helps us find joy in witnessing. There's no second guessing because God assures us whenever we share his word, it does not return to him empty (Isaiah 55:11). Instead, we watch with excitement and wonder to see what God will do next.

God could have taken us home to heaven the moment we came to faith, but he left us here in order to reach many more. I've heard countless Christians step into that role and wonder why they've waited so long. Like a puzzle piece that perfectly fits, they realize this was the reason we were made.

Paul, in 1 Corinthians 9, describes the blessings of witnessing. God doesn't just put his gospel into our hearts, but grace upon grace, he uses people like you to share it. We do it to "save some" (22). There is great joy in knowing God used you as a part of his eternal plan to reach a lost soul. Even if we don't see the results until heaven, we know God worked through us. Witnessing also allows us to share in the blessings of the gospel (23). You get a front row seat to the work of the Holy Spirit and sometimes have the privilege of seeing hearts and lives change right before your eyes. Like the farmer who sees the crop grow, you can't help but acknowledge the work of God in action. Finally, witnessing also blesses us personally so we are not "disqualified for the prize" (27). During the process, questions often come up that force you to dig deeper into the Word. You find even more answers in Christ. Witnessing leaves you with an even more profound appreciation for the gospel.

Don't underestimate the importance of your role.

> How, then can they call on the one they have not believed in? And how can they believe in the one of whom they have not heard? And how can they hear without someone preaching to them? And how can anyone preach unless they are sent? As it is written: 'How beautiful are the feet of those who bring good news!' (Romans 10:14-15)

God calls ordinary people to extraordinary work. Many of the first disciples were fishermen. Today, he uses people just like you to share it.

Luke was walking down the street when he stumbled and bumped into a pair of Mormon missionaries. This mistake was no accident. They developed a fast friendship and shared their beliefs. It broke Luke's heart. They talked about Jesus but didn't really know him. His concern grew. He thought, "I've got to do something about this."

Luke began to share the gospel with them. Early on, one of his friends was visibly moved and fought back tears. It was the first time he heard how much God loves him. Now he can't hear enough. The message began to draw others like a magnet. In a few short months, he was witnessing to 27 different Mormons. Luke shared: "No one is so far out grace can't reach them."

Luke understands the urgency as well as the importance for patience. He stays in touch with many of them weekly. He's answering their questions. They're walking together. While he has a day job, he would tell you his real calling now is a missionary. This journey has profoundly impacted his own faith. He has never experienced such joy.

Picture again the crumbling bridge of Mormonism. There are lost souls on that bridge trying to reach God. They are hoping their efforts will be enough. They don't realize the danger they face. They don't know the bridge God has already built to them. Yet.

You do. You're on God's bridge. You will safely cross the chasm. But don't run to the other side just yet. He didn't build this bridge for you to cross alone. He intends for you to reach back and invite still more. You can help Mormons discover the bridge to God. As you do, you'll find even more joy in the journey.

ADDITIONAL RESOURCES

ABOUT
TRUTH IN LOVE MINISTRY

Truth in Love Ministry is dedicated to speaking the truth of God's Word in love to Mormons.

OUR MISSION

Proclaiming Christ to Mormons —
Empowering Christians to Witness

Our approach is relational. We urge people to build bridges not barriers. We summarize our approach by the following five simple witnessing pillars:

1. See Mormons as victims, not enemies.
2. Treat Mormons with genuine love and respect.
3. Focus on Mormon stress points.
4. Speak the Mormon language.
5. Witness Christ rather than debate Mormonism.

Our ministry is supported by donations from friends like you. If you would like to support us, **visit tilm.org** or mail your gift to:

Truth in Love Ministry
1002 W Sanetta St
Nampa, ID 83651

DO YOU STRUGGLE WITH HOW TO SHARE YOUR FAITH?

We have a solution!

Our website, **tilm.org**, is full of free witnessing resources, video courses, downloadable guides, and so much more.

Explore our blog or enroll to receive our email updates and newsletters, full of witnessing tips and real-life stories of those impacted by our witnessing approach.

VISIT **TILM.ORG** TO LEARN MORE

EXPLORE HOW WE
WITNESS

Designed for LDS and those coming out of Mormonism, **BeYePerfect.org** is an example of our witnessing approach in action. This website speaks the Mormon language and addresses many topics which give Mormons stress.

The site is designed around questions LDS have about the truth and stories of those who have come to know that they are perfect in Christ.

We encourage you to share the articles on this site with your LDS friends to start a Christ-centered witnessing conversation.

GO TO **BEYEPERFECT.ORG**

ALSO AVAILABLE FROM
TRUTH IN LOVE MINISTRY

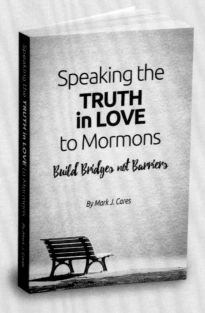

"An Insightful, Compassionate & Practical Approach."

Some Christians try to debate Mormons on topics like God's nature or the history or Mormonism. *Speaking the Truth in Love to Mormons* places the gospel of Jesus Christ at the center of discussion in witnessing. It has been transformational in helping many Christians better understand Mormons and how best to reach them.

VISIT **TILM.ORG/STORE**
TO ORDER YOUR COPY

ALSO AVAILABLE FROM
TRUTH IN LOVE MINISTRY

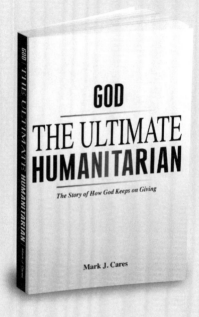

God's love is greater than anything we can imagine.

God is all powerful. He is all-knowing. He is eternal and so much more. God is truly incredible. *God—The Ultimate Humanitarian* considers 20 different facets of God's amazing love for humanity. It convincingly shows that God is the ultimate humanitarian.

VISIT **TILM.ORG/STORE**
TO ORDER YOUR COPY

INDEX

2 Corinthians 5:19 76, 89
2 Nephi 25:23 53, 54, 104

A

Agency 35
Atonement 53, 66, 67, 69, 74

B

Bible 13, 15, 28, 29, 32, 38, 44, 59, 62, 71, 86
Blessings 35, 57, 106

C

Commandments
    keep all the 35, 36, 37, 39, 43, 52, 53, 54, 56, 59, 75, 80, 81, 84, 89, 91
Conversion 85, 86
Covenants 15, 25, 58
Creditor 69, 70.
    See also LDS God

D

D&C 130:20-21 57
D&C 132:19-20 27

E

Eternal Life 25, 64, 71, 95, 104
Eternal Marriage 25, 26
Exaltation 25, 27, 59, 91
Exalted Man 25.
    See also LDS God
Example 71, 73, 88, 103.
    See also Jesus

F

Faith 57, 60, 78, 85, 87, 90, 91, 103
Fall 38, 40, 41, 61
Feelings 32, 81, 82, 103, 110
Forgiveness 54, 77, 82-89, 100, 109
Forsaketh His Sins 53, 82, 83

G

Gethsemane 67
Godhood 35, 36
Gods 27, 28, 35, 73
Grace 18, 53, 54, 56, 60, 61, 62, 68, 70, 74, 87, 88, 90, 100, 101, 102, 104, 105, 108, 109

H

Heaven 26, 43, 70, 75, 77, 101, 104, 109
Heavenly Mother 25, 26, 36
Holy Ghost 31, 80, 81, 82, 91
Holy Spirit 28, 59, 79, 86, 87, 90, 91, 92
Hope 97, 104, 105, 110

I

Identity 114-116

J

Jesus 31, 50, 54, 56, 59, 64, 65-77, 86, 89, 90, 91, 95, 100, 101, 103, 107, 110, 111
    example 73, 88, 103
    lived for us 74-76
    substitute 50, 73, 87, 103, 107, 110
John 5:22-23 72
Judgment Day 105, 110, 111

K

Kimball, Spencer W. 9, 56, 81, 83

L

Law 37, 38, 39, 42, 43, 44, 57, 76, 103, 107
LDS couplet 23, 34
LDS God 24, 25, 26
    creditor 69, 70
    Exalted Man 25
Listening 121, 122
Lived for Us 74.
    See also Jesus
Live Eternally with God 109

M

Matthew 5:48 55

N

Nature of God 122, 132

O

Obedience 35, 53, 54, 57, 67, 68, 69, 70
Only Begotten 65, 66
Ordinances 59, 67, 68, 101

P

Packer, Boyd K. 69
Perfection 36, 40, 56, 75, 76, 88, 99
perfect 37, 50, 55, 111, 123
Plan of Salvation 11, 52, 56, 57, 59, 70
Potential 33-39
Prayer 72
Preexistence 35
Progression 38, 55
Prophets 12, 16, 23
Purpose 25, 31, 36, 55, 56, 96, 107

R

Reconcile 76, 89
Repentance 82, 83, 84, 88, 89
Revelation 81-82
Romans 11:6 54, 60

S

Salvation 10, 52, 53, 54, 56, 59, 60, 61, 62, 64, 65, 68, 69, 70, 71, 73-76, 86, 90, 91, 110
saved 53, 60, 62, 67, 70, 74, 86, 90, 104
Savior 52, 65, 68-71, 100
Sin 21, 37-44, 51, 57, 61, 68, 69, 73, 75, 81, 82, 83, 84, 86, 89, 107, 117, 121, 124
Spirit Children 25, 36, 66
Spiritual Death 67
Spirit World 35, 101
Substitute
See Jesus

T

Testimony 103, 106
Testing 36
Trinity 28, 30, 31, 72
Trouble 96-100

W

Wilcox, Brad 70
Works 85, 89, 90
Worship 40, 72, 73
Worthy 26, 37, 53, 61, 80, 81, 86, 100

BIBLIOGRAPHY

Ballard, M. Russell. "Precious Gifts from God." *Ensign*, May 2018, p. 10.

The Holy Bible. Authorized King James Version with explanatory notes and cross references to the standard works of the Church of Jesus Christ of Latter-day Saints. The Church of Jesus Christ of Latter-day Saints, 2013.

The Book of Mormon: Another testament of Jesus Christ. The Church of Jesus Christ of Latter-day Saints, 2013.

Braun, Mark E. *Deuteronomy*, Northwestern Publishing House, 1993.

"Christ." *Bible Dictionary.* The Church of Jesus Christ of Latter-day Saints, 2013, p. 633.

Christofferson, D. Todd. "America's Changing Religious Landscape" *Ensign*, March 2020, p. 32.

Cooperman, Alan, et al. "What Church Leaders Are Saying about Why We Need the Church." *Pew Research Center's Religion & Public Life Project*, 7 May 2015, www.pewforum.org/2015/05/12/chapter-2-religious-switching-and-intermarriage/pr_15-05-12_rls_chapter2-02/.

Doctrine and Covenants. The Church of Jesus Christ of Latter-day Saints, 2013.

Doctrine and Covenants Instructor's Guide: Religion 324-325. E-book, The Church of Jesus Christ of Latter-day Saints, 1981.

Eyring, Henry B. "His Spirit to Be with You." *Ensign*, May 2018, p.86.

---. "Try, Try, Try." *Ensign*, Nov 2018, p. 90.

"Faith." *Bible Dictionary.* The Church of Jesus Christ of Latter-day Saints, 2013, p. 670.

Gospel Principles. The Church of Jesus Christ of Latter-day Saints, 2009.

Held, Mathias. "Seeking Knowledge by the Spirit." *Ensign*, May 2019, p. 32.

Hinckley, Gordon B. "The Family: A Proclamation to the World." General Relief Society Meeting, The Church of Jesus Christ of Latter-day Saints, 23 Sept. 1995, Salt Lake City, UT. Address.

---. "Mormon Should Mean 'More Good.'" *Ensign*, Nov 1990, p. 52.

Holland, Jeffrey R. "Be Ye Therefore Perfect—Eventually." *Ensign*, Nov 2017, p. 40.

Hymns of the Church of Jesus Christ of Latter-day Saints. The Church of Jesus Christ of Latter-day Saints, 1985.

"Mother in Heaven." *Gospel Topic Essays.* The Church of Jesus Christ of Latter-day Saints. www.churchofjesuschrist.org/study/manual/gospel-topics-essays/mother-in-heaven?lang=eng. Accessed 7 Feb. 2020.

Nelson, Russell M. "The Correct Name of the Church." *Ensign*, Nov 2018, p. 88.

---. "Divine Love." *Ensign*, Feb 2003, p.24.

---. "Let Us All Press On." *Ensign*, May 2018, p. 119.

Nelson, Wendy. *The Not Even Once Club.* Deseret Book Company, 2013.

Oaks, Dallin H. "Trust in the Lord." *Ensign*, Nov 2019, p. 22.

Pearl of Great Price. The Church of Jesus Christ of Latter-day Saints, 2013.

Pieper, Paul B. "All Must Take upon Them the Name Given of the Father." *Ensign*, Nov 2018, p. 45.

Plan of Salvation. The Church of Jesus Christ of Latter-day Saints, 2008.

"Prayer" *Bible Dictionary.* The Church of Jesus Christ of Latter-day Saints, 2013, p. 753.

Preach My Gospel. The Church of Jesus Christ of Latter-day Saints, 3rd ed., 2019.

Rasband, Ronald A. "Standing by our Promises and Covenants." *Ensign*, Nov 2019, p. 53.

Renlund, Dale G. "Abound with Blessings." *Ensign*, May 2019, p. 70.

Robbins, Lynn G. "Until Seventy Times Seven." *Ensign*, May 2018, p. 22.

Schaff, Philip. *The Person of Christ: The Miracle of History: With a Reply to Strauss and Renan, and a Collection of Testimonies of Unbelievers.* New York, Charles Scribner & Co, 1866.

Teachings of Presidents of the Church: Brigham Young. The Church of Jesus Christ of Latter-day Saints, 1997.

Teachings of Presidents of the Church: Joseph Smith. 2007. The Church of Jesus Christ of Latter-day Saints, 2011.

Teachings of Presidents of the Church: Joseph F. Smith. The Church of Jesus Christ of Latter-day Saints, 2011.

Teachings of Presidents of the Church: Joseph Fielding Smith. The Church of Jesus Christ of Latter-day Saints, 2013.

Teachings of Presidents of the Church: Lorenzo Snow. The Church of Jesus Christ of Latter-day Saints, 2012.

Teachings of Presidents of the Church: Spencer W. Kimball. The Church of Jesus Christ of Latter-day Saints, 2006.

True to the Faith. The Church of Jesus Christ of Latter-day Saints, 2004.

Uchtdorf, Dieter F. "A Yearning for Home." *Ensign*, Nov 2017, p. 24.

---. "Four Titles." *Ensign*, May 2013, p. 58.

---. "Your Great Adventure." *Ensign*, Nov 2019, p. 88.

"What is the Way to Eternal Life?" *Ensign*, Mar 2020, p. 43.

Wilcox, Brad. "His Grace is Sufficient." *Ensign*, Sept 2013, p. 35.

Yancey, Philip. *What's So Amazing About Grace.* Zondervan Publishing House, 1997.

ABOUT THE AUTHORS

Mark J. Cares is the former president of Truth in Love Ministry. He has been involved in mission work for over four decades: first as a mission pastor, then as a supervisor of missionaries. Throughout these years, he has witnessed to thousands of Mormons and has equipped thousands of Christians to witness. He is the author of *Speaking the Truth in Love to Mormons* and *God—The Ultimate Humanitarian*. He and his wife, Bonnie, have five children and twelve grandchildren.

Jon Leach has served as a mission pastor, cross-cultural mission instructor and missionary. He shares his contagious passion for the lost as a writer, speaker and mentor. He has master's degrees in both divinity and intercultural missional leadership. He has led world mission teams and currently serves as president of Truth in Love Ministry. He and his wife, Liz, have four boys and reside in Nampa, Idaho.

We are therefore Christ's ambassadors, as though
God were making his appeal through us.

2 Corinthians 5:20